The West of Buffalo Bill

The West of
Buffalo Bill

Frontier Art, Indian Crafts,
Memorabilia from the
Buffalo Bill Historical Center

HARRY N. ABRAMS, INC. PUBLISHERS
NEW YORK

Margaret L. Kaplan, *Managing Editor*
Nai Y. Chang, *Vice President, Design*
Prof. Sam Hunter, Princeton University, *Editorial Consultant*
Patricia Gilchrest, *Editor*
Betty Binns, *Book Design*

Library of Congress Cataloging in Publication Data
Main entry under title:
The West of Buffalo Bill; frontier art, Indian crafts,
memorabilia from the Buffalo Bill Historical Center.
1. Buffalo Bill Historical Center. 2. The West in art.
I. McCracken, Harold, 1894–
E56.W47   917.8'03'074018742   74-5357
ISBN 0-8109-0219-2

Contents

Rosa Bonheur. *Colonel
William F. Cody.* 1889.
Oil, 18 x 14″

Introduction

THE maze of highways that each season brings hundreds of thousands of summer vacationers from all parts of the United States to visit Yellowstone National Park eventually converges into the east entrance of that greatest of all concentrations of natural phenomena, scenic wonders, and wild life. In the small town of Cody, Wyoming, at the edge of the Rocky Mountains, where all the roads join to enter the nearby park, the traveler encounters what is probably the most imposing building seen on the journey from Florida, Pennsylvania, or Maine. Standing on a forty-acre plot of land, facing the main highway, is the two-million dollar structure that houses the museum complex of the Buffalo Bill Historical Center. The building, which sprawls over an area longer than two professional football fields, is constructed entirely of native stone and reinforced concrete, is completely air-conditioned, and is equipped according to the most modern museum standards. This impressive and dignified building contains what has been internationally recognized as one of the largest and finest public displays of authentic materials relating to the early frontier days on the Northern Plains and in the adjoining Rocky Mountain area. Strictly an educational, nonprofit undertaking dedicated to investigating, preserving, and displaying the Old West as it really was, the center has over a period of more than half a century grown to a ten-million-dollar institution, although, significantly, it is not supported by city, state, or federal funds. The entire project is a classic example of that nearly lost spirit of rugged individualism and independent enterprise which was the basic motivation in the early development of the American West.

The center is obviously a memorial to the most famous and glamorous of the early Western frontiersmen, Col. William F. "Buffalo Bill" Cody; and it is only natural that this broadly oriented memorial should be in the town which he founded and which bears his name.

The genesis of this extensive center of Western Americana was in January 1917, about two weeks after Buffalo Bill's death. A group of his friends and admirers who were residents of Cody, which was near to his sprawling TE cattle ranch, decided that something should be done to preserve the memory of their world-famous friend, who had done so much for the development and benefit of the region in which he made his home. In semiretirement Buffalo Bill was universally recognized as the one man whose name was synonymous with the rough and rugged glamour of the Western American frontier. In his boyhood days he crossed the Great Plains with the slow-moving freight wagons. Later he served as a professional buffalo hunter to feed the railroad builders, then became chief of scouts for the Indian-fighting U.S. Cavalry. As the flamboyant impresario of his big Wild West show, he took the exciting story of earlier days to millions of people in both the United States and Europe. He had led a spectacular life in the forefront of events and had probably done more than anyone else to create a world-wide image of rugged Americanism. He was the friend of at least one president of the United States, and played host on stagecoach rides to at least five of the crowned heads of European countries, several of whom had personally entertained him and given him lavish gifts. Hundreds of nickel-and-dime paperback books had been written about his exploits and translated into a dozen foreign languages, although many of them were without foundation in fact and did him more lasting harm than good.

But there is another and far less publicized side to the life of this man, as is the case with some of our entertainment personalities today. It is often true that the Hollywood sex symbol and "villain" are not what their public images imply. This was, to a large extent, true of Buffalo Bill. He was certainly flamboyant and spectacularly histrionic in the important part he played in the taming of the West. But there is another aspect of his character. For example, Sitting Bull was his staunch friend. For many years the chief carried as one of his most cherished possessions a small framed photograph of the two of them standing together, and he wore a gold ring that Buffalo Bill had given him. (Both of these articles are on display in the Buffalo Bill Historical Center.) Many historians say that if Cody had been able to complete his mission to Sitting Bull at the Standing Rock Agency in 1890 before the chief was inadvertently killed, the Wounded Knee massacre would have been avoided. Cody invested millions of dollars of the profits from his Wild West Show in the economic development of projects from Arizona to Wyoming. He was the first to promote tourism and commercial ventures in connection with Yellowstone National Park. And he was generous to a fault in giving money to relatives and friends.

Through his friendship with President Theodore Roosevelt Cody was responsible for the first major project of the U.S. Bureau of Reclamation, the building of the Buffalo Bill Dam, which was made possible through the Reclamation Act of 1902. The dam, which controlled the waters of the Shoshone River, was completed in 1909. The 328-foot high structure was built "by man, mules and shovels" and for several years was the

Aerial view of the Buffalo Bill Historical Center

The Buffalo Bill Historical Center, Cody, Wyoming

highest dam in the world. It supplied irrigation for three hundred thousand acres of farmland and furnished electricity for the entire area. Buffalo Bill never personally benefited in any way from this project, but after well over half a century it benefits far more of his fellow citizens than originally expected.

The greatest irony in the Buffalo Bill story is the fact that when he died at the beginning of 1917 he was practically penniless and in debt. But he was deeply respected and loved by those who knew him best as one of our greatest ambassadors of rugged Americanism. As Theodore Roosevelt said: "He embodied those traits of courage, strength, and self-reliant hardihood which are so vital to the well-being of our nation." This fact was recognized by his fellow townspeople, who in 1917 became determined to create a memorial to this extraordinary man.

Using the name Buffalo Bill Memorial Association, the Cody group requested and was granted a charter under the laws of the State of Wyoming as a charitable trust, to "build and maintain a historical monument . . . to William F. Cody 'Buffalo Bill' . . . for the preservation of the history of the country." Although there was not much available in the way of funds, plans were begun toward building a museum to house Colonel

Gertrude Vanderbilt Whitney. *Buffalo Bill Cody—the Scout* (two views). 1923. Bronze, H. 12′ 5″

William Frederick Cody, 1876

William Frederick Cody in 1895 at the
height of his career with the Wild West
Show

Cody's personal effects in the hope that these historic memorabilia might be kept together and preserved. There were hundreds of items—jeweled gifts from European royalty, finely beaded war shirts from famous Indian chiefs, guns, and a large collection of paintings by some of the country's best-known artists. Among others, Cody's long-time friend Frederic Remington had on a number of occasions been a guest at the big TE ranch, with its herds of cattle and cowboy veterans of the Wild West Show. A sizeable Remington painting given to Cody today hangs in the Buffalo Bill museum.

Friends and relatives of Colonel Cody contributed other items that had belonged to the colorful frontiersman. The collection grew in a very satisfactory manner and was carefully stored until the time when there would be enough money available to construct a museum.

Buffalo Bill had a great host of admirers in high places, ranging from Gen. Nelson A. Miles to the Grand Duke Alexis of Russia and Gertrude Vanderbilt Whitney. It was Mrs. Whitney, the socialite sculptor of international renown, who created the heroic equestrian bronze statue *Buffalo Bill Cody—the Scout*, depicting him on his favorite horse. On July 4, 1924, this statue was ceremoniously unveiled in the town of Cody and presented to the Buffalo Bill Memorial Association. Shortly after this the gracious lady acquired the forty-acre piece of land on which the statue had been placed, and donated it for the development of the Buffalo Bill Historical Center. Today this statue is one of the best-known and most photographed equestrian statues in the United States.

It was exactly three years later, on July 4, 1927, largely through the efforts of Mary Jester Allen, a devoted niece of Colonel Cody, and with the assistance of Mrs. Whitney and other generous persons, that the Buffalo Bill Museum was opened to the public. It was housed in a newly built log cabin alongside the highway into Yellowstone Park. Mary Jester Allen, a member of the Cody family who had been associated with Buffalo Bill in the management of the Wild West Show, was particularly fitted to be curator of the new museum. She served in this capacity with indefatigable dedication and almost on a charity basis until her death in 1960.

It was not until April 25, 1959, that the first large and modern museum building was dedicated and opened to the public, on the forty acres that had so long before been provided by Mrs. Whitney. The half-million-dollar fund for this building was allocated from the Gertrude Vanderbilt Whitney Trust by the Honorable Cornelius Vanderbilt Whitney, to commemorate his late mother's high regard for Colonel Cody and her devotion to American art. The new museum building, appropriately named the Whitney Gallery of Western Art, was devoted to the early documentary artists of the Old West, such as Frederic Remington, Charles M. Russell, Albert Bierstadt, and others. It was decided that in the future the collections of the Historical Center would be primarily regional in scope.

It was by coincidence that I became director of the Whitney Gallery and the fledgling Historical Center. During the late summer and fall of 1958, the big stone building for the new museum was in the process of being completed. At this time I was staying at a dude ranch near the town of Cody, completing my book *George Catlin and the Old Frontier*. The ranch was operated by a long-time friend who was a member of the

Gertrude Vanderbilt Whitney in her studio in 1923 with her heroic sculpture *Buffalo Bill Cody—the Scout.* The statue was later permanently installed in Cody, Wyoming

Mary Jester Allen (niece of Buffalo Bill and founder of the Buffalo Bill Museum). 1957. Relief

board of trustees of the Buffalo Bill Memorial Association. Having enjoyed the successful publication of my books *Frederic Remington—Artist of the Old West* and *The Charles M. Russell Book,* and having long been involved with the field of Western art, I was naturally interested in the plans and problems of the new Cody museum and had entered into a number of discussions with members of the board and made certain recommendations. I had been asked to take over the directorship, but for several reasons I was not interested. After many years of disappointing struggle my books were finally doing surprisingly well. The interest in Western art was just beginning to become widespread (my books on Remington and Russell had provided evidence of this trend and had perhaps contributed to it), and I was intent on continuing my writing. While the association had an awesomely large building, there was nothing to put into it, and no funds were available for purchases. The whole thing seemed a rather hopeless situation.

However, while my wife and I were at the Cody Airport waiting for the plane to take us back to our home on Long Island, two members of the board arrived there. They urged me to return to Cody as soon as my Catlin book was in the hands of the

The Original Buffalo Bill Museum in Cody, Wyoming

Dr. Harold McCracken opening the door of the Buffalo Bill Historical Center after the cutting of the ribbon at dedication ceremonies, May 31, 1969

publisher and accept the responsibilities of becoming director of the Whitney Gallery of Western Art and the Buffalo Bill Historical Center. Somehow, just before we got onto the plane, I agreed to the proposal. All the way back to New York I wondered why I had committed myself to such a seemingly hopeless undertaking. I tried desperately to convince myself that this was a challenge worthy of anyone's best efforts and that the opportunity was the sort that comes to very few individuals in a lifetime.

As soon as I got back to New York I went to work. The finding of good exhibition material was certainly the only hope. Through my years of involvement in the field I had made a lot of friends among both dealers and important collectors, and I went to them for help. From the very beginning the response was beyond my most optimistic hopes. The idea of a big museum devoted to the art of the Old West had a genuine appeal, and the Whitney name helped a lot. Nearly every dealer and collector I contacted was willing to lend the best of their paintings and bronzes to help get the project started. Also, men of means liked the idea of independent enterprise.

I was back in Cody on January 19, 1959, and was asked to meet the president of the board at the museum. The building contractor was also there. In a brief, informal ceremony the contractor turned over to the president of the board a large bunch of keys, which was in turn promptly handed to me, with the rather terse comment, "Well …it's all up to you now. We have planned to have the dedication and opening on May 1." Then the two of them left me alone. I guess it was then that I officially became the director. But I felt very much alone, as I looked around the very big and painfully vacant interior, with its shiny terrazzo floor and its 840 feet of high, bare walls. A cold chill came over me as I wondered if there would ever be enough Western art to make a reasonable showing on all that bare wall space; and then I wondered if anyone would come to see the pictures, if the pictures really materialized. In a little Western town of five thousand people it all seemed quite impossible. There was only a telephone on a makeshift table in the very small office, which had been used by the contractor. I had no secretary and had to find a janitor who could handle the elaborate heating and air-conditioning plant.

However, I soon learned that the Honorable Robert Coe, a member of the board, and his W. R. Coe Foundation had arranged to acquire the Frederic Remington Studio Collection, consisting of 109 oil sketches and unfinished paintings and more than a thousand articles of fine Indian costumes, cowboy gear, and early pioneer material the famous artist had collected on his various Western travels between 1880 and 1907. This extremely important material was sufficient to fill one forty-foot-square alcove of the museum. My longtime good friend William Davidson, then of the Knoedler Galleries in New York, who had handled the transaction of the Remington Studio Collection, had agreed to come to Cody with two assistants to supervise the building of cases and set up the entire display. This was the beginning of a snowball that grew and grew as if by magic.

The next good news was that William E. Weiss, a board member, had acquired, through William Davidson, a very large and important collection of Charles M. Russell paintings and bronzes which he planned to lend to the Whitney Gallery. Then boxes and crates began arriving by air express and surface transportation from various parts of the country. This generosity was climaxed by the dispatching from New York City of a large moving van containing $1,500,000 worth of Western art, which Bill Davidson had gathered together with the cooperation of Rudolf Wunderlich of Kennedy Galleries and other New York dealers. After having daily telephone contact with the big van and its precious load as it moved across the country over the icy roads of late winter, we finally saw it roll up in front of the museum door, in a blinding Wyoming snowstorm.

Although the dedication and opening date was moved forward to April 25 to accommodate the schedule of the principal benefactor, the walls of the big Whitney Gallery were amply hung with fine Western art in time for the auspicious occasion; thus the seemingly impossible had been accomplished.

Three large planes had been chartered to bring dignitaries and newspapermen to Cody from New York and California; one of the planes, however, was unable to make a landing at the small Cody Airport because of bad weather. The opening of the gallery got a surprising amount of advance publicity—more than 2,500 visitors attended the opening and tracked mud all over the beautiful terrazzo floor (every square inch of which was dear to the director!); and the many newspaper reports on the new museum were a delight. *New York Times:* "The Gertrude Vanderbilt Whitney Gallery is a magnificent documentation of a dramatic subject . . . pure West. Cowboys, mountain men, Indians . . . . There has never been a more comprehensive exhibit of Western Americana anywhere." *Los Angeles Times:* "An extraordinary exhibit of Western Americana . . . . Anyone planning to visit Yellowstone Park should not miss this." *San Francisco Chronicle:* "A suitable national repository for a comprehensive and factual pictorial record of the Old West...one of the most important assemblages of Western Americana art that has been gathered together." And there were others equally laudatory.

We had enough visitors that first season to pay for the museum's operation and maintenance from the small admission charge. Being at the converging point of all highways leading into the nearby east entrance to Yellowstone Park was from the beginning a great advantage to the museum, and each succeeding year the attendance increased considerably. Each year the permanent collection also increased; and it was not very long before it became obvious that in the foreseeable future the gallery which had once seemed so cavernous would be entirely too small for the purpose for which it was intended.

In the meantime the old Buffalo Bill Museum remained rather dormant, in its deteriorating log building on the other side of the highway. The fact that the irreplaceable memorabilia of the famous frontiersman were housed in an antiquated structure that was a serious fire hazard was a cause for increasing concern. Furthermore, the collections of exceptionally fine Plains Indian materials had increased to such an extent that the majority of them had to be kept packed away in the storage rooms in the basement of the Whitney Gallery. Also, for several years the center had been carrying on archaeological work in the surrounding area, culminating in the excavation of a mountain cave near the boundary of Yellowstone Park. The work on the cave, which was financed by two substantial grants from the National Geographic Society, resulted

Entrance foyer of the Buffalo Bill Historical Center

The Buffalo Bill Museum in the Buffalo Bill Historical Center

in the discovery of the well-preserved mummified body of a Stone Age cave man of the high Rocky Mountains, along with important cultural artifacts going back more than nine thousand years. These accumulated circumstances indicated the necessity for additional exhibition space at least three times as large as the space provided by the Whitney Gallery of Western Art.

Several programs had been initiated to raise funds for the construction of a new and fireproof Buffalo Bill Museum on the forty acres, but none of these plans had been successful, largely because of the national economic situation. In the meantime it was decided best to aim for a museum complex to be housed under a single roof, adding the necessary space to the Whitney Gallery. With this in mind architectural drawings were made. The cost of the project was estimated at $1,200,000, not including the extensive bronze finishings and display cases. Money was pledged, including a sum that averaged close to a hundred dollars per person for the five thousand residents of Cody. But the total amount collected fell far below what was needed to even begin the building. Then one of the members of the board got an idea. This was Peter Kriendler, the majordomo of the famous "21" Club in New York City. He suggested to Winchester-Western Company that they manufacture a Buffalo Bill commemorative rifle and donate a liberal royalty to the nonprofit Buffalo Bill Memorial Association to be used in constructing the new building. The idea was a natural one. The Winchester had for more than a century been known as "the Gun That Won the West," and it was equally well known that it had been Buffalo Bill Cody's favorite rifle. Buffalo Bill's grandson Fred Garlow was also a member of the board. Dressed in the famous frontiersman's characteristic attire, Garlow liberally participated in the dignified promotion of the commemorative rifle. The plan proved to be a tremendous success, and the royalties donated by Winchester-Western were responsible for the new building becoming a reality. The elaborate dedication and opening ceremonies were held on May 31, 1969, with Dr. John Walker, director of the National Gallery of Art in Washington, D.C., giving the principal dedicatory address. That same afternoon and evening more than five thousand guests attended the ceremonies and viewed under one roof the exhibits of the Whitney Gallery of Western Art, the Buffalo Bill Museum, and the Plains Indian Museum.

Since the opening of the new building, the Historical Center has become widely recognized as one of the truly great museum complexes of its kind. The annual attendance for the summer period between May 1 and September 30 has climbed to 225,000 visitors. Thus it has become known to those who shape the destiny of the Buffalo Bill Historical Center that the seemingly impossible can be realized even today by independent enterprise, and future plans for further development are in the making.

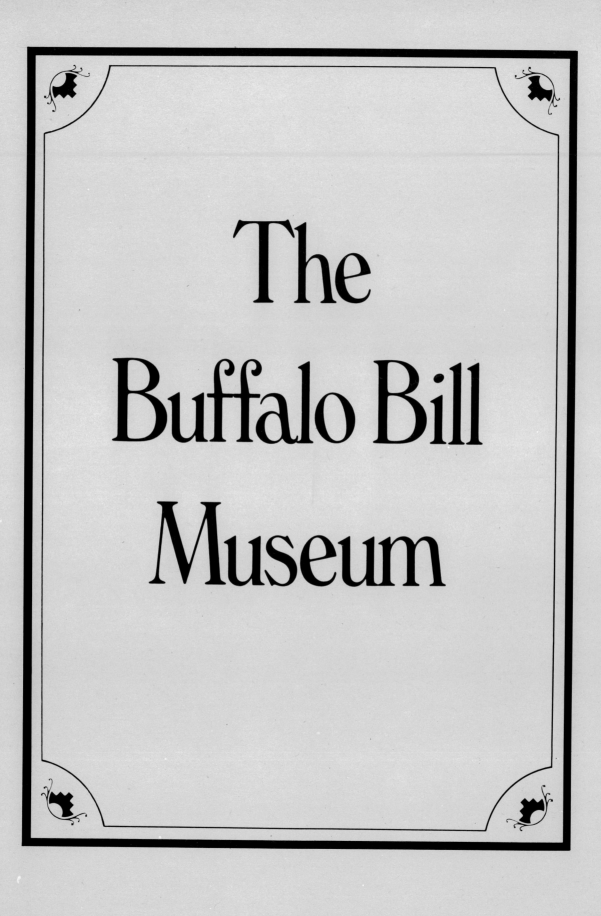

The Buffalo Bill Museum

Irving R. Bacon. Detail of *Conquest of the Prairie*. 1908. Oil, 48 x 120" *(foldout)*

HE best-known American of his age, the world over" was a remark often made about Col. William F. "Buffalo Bill" Cody at the turn of the last century. Nearly fifty books have recounted the life of the famous scout, buffalo hunter, and master showman—some accurately, others less so. These have been translated into a dozen languages and avidly read by younger generations of almost every nationality. Seventeen hundred issues of adventure pulps, weekly magazines, Beadle half-dime novels, and soft-cover fiction by Col. Prentiss Ingraham and others may be added to the store of Buffalo Bill truth and legend. Few authors, however, have treated Cody with the honesty and fidelity of his own attempts to document the Old West and various events in his life.

More than forty years of public appearances, first on the theater circuit and later with his great Wild West Show, have endeared Cody to several generations. Repeated tours to every part of this country and Europe brought an educational and historic portrayal of the American West to millions. Even today Buffalo Bill is as much a hero in Europe as he is in his native land.

This exposure, greater than that of almost any other American citizen, cannot in itself account for the public regard that Colonel Cody received in his day, and that has flourished since his death.

A combination of the events of the time and personal characteristics is perhaps responsible for the prominent place Cody holds in our national heritage. Born in the mid-nineteenth century, in the final, exciting phase of this country's development and struggle for unity, he contributed to every phase of its early growth, as he later did to the development of the frontier West. The stamina, horsemanship, courage, and intelligence he displayed as a boy rider with the Pony Express continued through years of scouting the Plains Indians and accurately guiding the military. Senior officers with whom he served as scout recognized the value of his absolute dependability, his marksmanship, and his rare ability to recall completely the features of terrain he had perhaps seen only once, years earlier. The same qualities contributed to Cody's skill as a hunter who provided meat for the crews of the Kansas Pacific Railroad, and inspired the respect shown him by Indians who had personal knowledge of this extraordinary man.

An intense patriotism was felt by the young Cody. Pride in the land of his birth directed his actions throughout his life. Optimistic by nature, totally lacking in fear, he had the confidence and determination needed to surmount the difficulties and responsibilities that confronted him throughout his career. Cody had the happy faculty of being able to laugh at himself. He was willing to share the worst as well as the best with commoners and royalty alike.

In later life he espoused the cause of conservation and fostered reclamation, irrigation, road-building, and recreation for the community that he founded and developed in Wyoming.

Don Russell, an outstanding student of Cody, writes in his book *The Lives and Legends of Buffalo Bill:* "In an age that is skeptical of heroism, anyone who does bother to find out what William F. Cody really amounted to may turn up a record that is impressive in its universal acclaim from a wide variety of sources, as well as in its lack of any hint that he ever faltered or blundered. What more could be asked of a hero? If he was not one, who was?"

Assembling the collections of the Buffalo Bill Museum began very shortly after Cody's death in 1917 and is still continuing. Purchases by the Buffalo Bill Memorial Association and gifts from the estate of Colonel Cody and from family members account for the bulk of personal items, paintings, posters, guns, furniture, stage coaches, and other memorabilia housed in the museum. Gifts and cash contributions from friends of Buffalo Bill have increased the whole to more than twenty-five thousand items, so that the total constitutes one of the greatest personal collections of its sort in history.

William F. Cody was born on February 26, 1846, in a log cabin, following the best American tradition. His parents, Isaac and Mary Ann Laycock Cody, were living near LeClaire, Scott County, Iowa, having been married in Cincinnati in 1840. Bill was the third of six children. The older son, Sam, was killed by a fall from a horse at the age of twelve, and Bill shared family responsibilities with Julia, his older sister, and the younger girls, Eliza Alice, Laura Ella, and Mary Hannah. His playground was the west bank of the Mississippi River, the launching area for overland expeditions westward.

After the tragic death of their older son, the family moved to Kansas, where Isaac, a free-state man, was stabbed by a proslavery adversary while making an antislavery speech. This injury resulted in Isaac's death three years later, and Bill Cody became the man of the family at the age of eleven. The responsibility placed on him at that time remained with him all his life, and he provided well for his family during the next sixty years.

Little formal education was available to the Codys on the frontier, and Bill's school days ended in the fourth grade. Thereafter, practical training, experience, and personal relationships provided him with the means to succeed.

The lure of the vast Western frontier was particularly strong for young Bill Cody, and after his father died he signed as a messenger boy with the wagon trains of Majors and Russell. The firm held contracts to supply the armies on the Plains, and their freight teams of oxen and heavy wagons traveled across the West in great numbers. Ever since gold had been found in California, the migration westward had continually increased. The Oregon Trail, now well established, carried such a volume of traffic that Indian tribes were waging continual war against the whites, for they felt that their hunting grounds and way of life were in danger of destruction. Army units were thinly deployed in an effort to protect long routes of migration. Bill Cody learned much about the ways of the Indian and the lay of the land while riding with the supply trains.

As our West Coast areas began to be settled, demands were made for better communication with Eastern centers of commerce. Ships pushing south around Cape Horn and up the long Western coastline took months to deliver news. For this reason the Pony Express was born. Bill's firm, now called Russell, Majors and Waddell, undertook the difficult task of launching that daring operation.

Hundreds of fast horses were gathered, scores of stations set up, routes determined, and young men with sinewy bodies and great courage were engaged for the Pony Express. The long eighteen hundred miles from St. Joseph, Missouri, to Sacramento, California, were covered in 10 exhausting days, with 190 changes of horse. Through mountainous and Indian-infested country, snow and heat, the express operated from April 1860 until November 1861, when the telegraph was completed. What a feat it was! Although of short duration, the Pony Express was an epic chapter in our history.

Bill Cody, at fifteen years of age, was a rider with the Pony Express. He made one of the record rides from Three Crossings to Rocky Ridge and back—over three hundred and twenty miles (on twenty-two different horses) in less than twenty-two hours, reaching every station on time! Training of this kind proved valuable for Cody's later services as an Indian scout for the military.

After the death of his mother in the winter of 1863, young Cody enlisted in the Union Army, joining the Seventh Kansas Volunteer Cavalry. He served in several engagements against the Confederates and was mustered out with a creditable record in the fall of 1865.

Louisa Frederici, the daughter of a French father and an American mother, and a devout Catholic girl living in the French section of St. Louis, met young Bill Cody while he was on military duty there near the end of the Civil War. After a short courtship,

Buffalo Bill's boyhood home. Moved in 1933 from Iowa to Cody, Wyoming;
relocated near the Buffalo Bill Historical Center in 1970

they were married on March 6, 1866. He took his bride immediately to Fort Leavenworth, where employment as a scout for the U.S. Army awaited him.

Cody's knowledge of the frontier country and its Indian inhabitants, along with his willingness to volunteer for hazardous assignments, soon advanced him to the position of chief scout for the Fifth United States Cavalry. Later testimonials by Generals Sheridan, Carr, Miles, and other military leaders point up the extraordinary services performed by scout Cody. One such incident of heroism occurred in July 1869, during the Battle of Summit Springs. Cody, who was guiding Gen. Eugene A. Carr's forces, helped rescue a white woman held captive by Indians. This encounter was the subject of one of Charles Schreyvogel's great paintings, *The Summit Springs Rescue*. The painting was acquired by Cody years later and is now hanging in the Buffalo Bill Historical Center.

General Sheridan, at Fort Hays, Kansas, gave out the following statement after receiving messages carried by Cody from Fort Larned sixty-five miles away:

> The intelligence received required that certain orders should be carried to Fort Dodge, ninety-five miles south of Hays. This too being a particularly dangerous route—several couriers having been killed on it—it was impossible to get one of the various "Petes," "Jacks," or "Jims," hanging around Hays City to take my communication. Cody, learning of the strait I was in, manfully came to the rescue, and proposed to make the trip to Dodge, though he had just finished his long and perilous ride from Larned. I gratefully accepted his offer, and after four or five hours' rest he mounted a fresh horse and hastened on his journey, halting but once to rest on the way, and then only for an hour, the stop being made at Coon Creek, where he got another mount from a troop of cavalry. At Dodge, he took six hours' sleep, and then continued on to his own post—Fort Larned—with more dispatches. After resting twelve hours at Larned, he was again in the saddle with tidings for me at Fort Hays, General Hazen sending him, this time, with word that the [Indian] villages had fled to the south of the Arkansas. Thus, in all, Cody rode about 350 miles in less than sixty hours, and such an exhibition of endurance and courage was more than enough to convince me that his services would be extremely valuable in the campaign, so I retained him at Fort Hays till the battalion of the Fifth Cavalry arrived, and then made him chief of scouts for that regiment.

During periods of relative quiet and between military campaigns, Cody turned his talents to hunting buffalo. He earned the name "Buffalo Bill" for his skill in this endeavor and was considered the best of the many professional buffalo hunters. Cody's .50-caliber Springfield rifle, nicknamed Lucretia Borgia, and his favorite horse, Brigham, which had a natural bent for running buffalo, were a combination unequaled on the plains. While employed by the Kansas Pacific Railroad to supply meat for its crew of twelve hundred track-layers, Buffalo Bill delivered over four thousand buffalo in eight months.

It is generally recognized that the "hide-hunter" and his crew of skinners were responsible for the decimation of the buffalo in the decade 1873–83. Such irresponsible destruction reduced the Plains Indians, who depended on the buffalo for food and other necessities, from a free, proud people to impoverished wards of the govern-

Buffalo Bill at the age of eleven, 1857

E. Z. C. Judson (Ned Buntline),
author, c. 1875

William Cary. *Scout Cody Guiding the Army.* c. 1875. Etching, 9 x 16″

Royal jewelry given to Colonel Cody during his continental tours: buffalo-head rings and scarf pin from the Grand Duke Alexis of Russia; blue-enameled diamond ring from Kaiser Wilhelm II of Germany; diamond crown watch from King Victor Emmanuel of Italy; watch engraved with buffalo chase from King Edward VII of England; diamond brooch fob from Queen Victoria of England

Museum exhibit showing Buffalo Bill with the Czar of Russia's fur robe, a gift to Cody following the royal buffalo hunt, which he guided in 1872

The Wild West Show flag

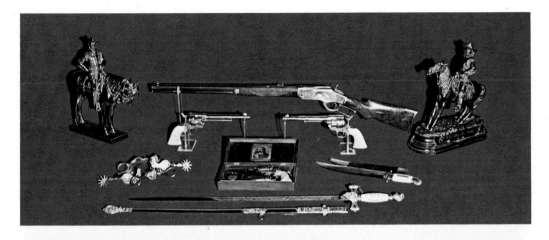

Museum exhibit of Cody weapons. Top to bottom: 1873 Winchester, caliber .44; pair of Colt Frontier revolvers, engraved, nickle-plated, with ivory handles; brass and nickel spurs and bit made for Cody (left); 1860 Colt pocket pistol, caliber .36 (center); Bowie knife with Cody's signature (right); Knights Templar sword and scabbard (bottom). On either side of the display are bronzes of Cody by Amory Simons (1905; left), and Philibert Claitte (1907; right)

Museum exhibit showing Buffalo Bill and the famous Deadwood Stagecoach

Museum exhibit showing Colonel Cody, his saddle, and a 1908 poster by the Strobridge Lithograph Company of Cincinnati and New York

G. H. Stephens. *Hunting Buffalo.* c. 1880–90. Oil, 18 x 24″

ment. Cody, however, was never one to slaughter animals wantonly. He championed the conservation of the buffalo in later years, and his own small herd proved valuable to that end.

Col. E. Z. C. Judson, better known as Ned Buntline, writer, actor, and temperance lecturer, made his appearance on the Kansas prairies during this period. Hearing about young Buffalo Bill and his reputation, Judson wrote the first of the fictional Buffalo Bill stories, which led to a flood of others, and to the beginning of the wide renown of Buffalo Bill.

Cody's fame as a hunter resulted in his frequent detachment from military duties for the purpose of guiding distinguished visitors from the East on buffalo and big-game hunts. Sir John Watts Garland and the Earl of Dunraven from England, along with Easterners James Gordon Bennett, Charles L. Wilson, Lawrence and Leonard Jerome, and Professor Othniel Charles Marsh of Yale University, were some of the notables who hunted with Buffalo Bill as their guide in 1871-72.

In the fall of 1871 Czar Alexander II of Russia sent his son the Grand Duke Alexis to the United States on a good-will mission. While touring the country, Alexis expressed a desire to hunt buffalo on the Western Plains. General Philip Sheridan, in charge of the excursion, designated General George Armstrong Custer and Buffalo Bill to organize an elaborate hunt. Chief Spotted Tail, with his group of Sioux, agreed to entertain the royal guest with Indian dances and a bow-and-arrow buffalo hunt. Leaving the duke's special train at North Platte, Nebraska, the party, including a large press contingent, journeyed to Red Willow Creek in army wagons and enjoyed a spectacular and successful hunt. Alexis, astride Buffalo Bill's horse Buckskin Joe, killed his first buffalo and had many thrills. Much publicity was given to the outing, and Cody received his first gifts from a member of the European nobility. Paintings and drawings of this famous hunt were done by Charles M. Russell and other prominent Western artists.

In 1872 Buffalo Bill was elected to the state legislature of Nebraska. (He had moved his family to Fort McPherson in 1870.) He never served in that post, but he did use the title associated with the office, "Honorable," in future publicity. The same year he was awarded the United States Medal of Honor for the courage he had displayed in a fight with Indians during the summer. The medal was rescinded, however, many years later when Congress ruled that recipients must be officers or enlisted men of the military, and called back all medals that had been issued to civilians.

Buffalo Bill's former hunting companions, Ned Buntline in particular, prevailed on him to make his first visit to the East in the fall of 1872. While there, Cody was taken by Buntline to a play the latter had written, and the writer persuaded Cody to play the lead in other productions. Texas Jack Omohundro, a friend and army scout, joined Cody in the acting venture, and their initial appearance was in Chicago in December. The plays were woefully short on acting and finesse, and long on improvisation and ineptness. Critics were most unkind, but the audiences loved the acts and the action. For the next dozen years Cody continued to appear in productions during the winter season. These performances may have given birth to our popular "Western" of television and the movies. They were also a probable source of inspiration for Cody's great Wild West Show, which was to evolve a few years later.

James "Wild Bill" Hickok, famed lawman and scout, joined the cast of the Buffalo Bill Combination for a time, but lost favor with the troupe when he repeatedly powder-burned the legs of actors playing the roles of Indians with shots from his Colt .44. He and Cody had been friends as scouts and had served in the Union Army together, but Hickok was too restless and action-loving to remain in the theater.

In early June of 1876, Cody left the stage in New York and reported to his old army command under General Carr, at Cheyenne, Wyoming. He guided a group of officers, General Sheridan among them, to the Red Cloud Indian reservation, while Generals Terry, Gibbon, and Custer were moving against the warring Sioux to the north. Thus Buffalo Bill missed the massacre of Custer's troops at Little Big Horn, although he served as scout with part of the same command. A few weeks later, guiding Colonel Merritt, commander of the Fifth Cavalry, Cody killed a Cheyenne subchief called Yellow Hand between the lines of hostile Sioux and the army. This incident, later reported in different versions by a variety of sources, became known as "the First Scalp for Custer" or "the Yellow Hand Duel." Army records document the episode and Buffalo Bill's principal part in the affair.

To punish the Indians after the Custer fight, a large command was put together called the Big Horn and Yellowstone Expedition, and Bill Cody was made chief of

"Welcome Wigwam," Buffalo Bill's home in North Platte, Nebraska

George A. Custer, the Grand Duke Alexis of
Russia, and Buffalo Bill at the time of the
great royal buffalo hunt, 1872

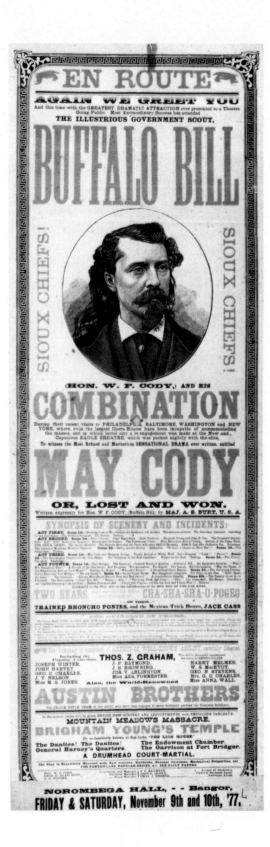

May Cody, or Lost and Won. Advertisement for stage plays presented by the Buffalo Bill Combination, 1872–75.

scouts for that force. The Sioux were pursued hotly, until, under pressure, they broke into small groups and disappeared into the hills and mountains. This expedition ended Cody's service as paid government scout. He spent the next few years performing in his Buffalo Bill Combination, with considerable financial success and acclaim.

Cody also devoted much time to developing his Scout's Rest Ranch and cattle and horse interests at North Platte, Nebraska, which he had acquired in 1877. It was there, in the spring of 1882, that his neighbors and ranch friends persuaded him to stage a local Fourth of July celebration. That date was of special significance to Cody, and he never failed to observe it throughout his life. The Independence Day celebration which he planned for North Platte was to be an outdoor entertainment suited to the tastes of the people of the area. Bronco busting, horse racing, riding feats, and shooting exhibitions were part of the program. Handbills were printed and circulated to attract both contestants and audience. Much was promised, prizes were announced, and the thinly populated country responded for miles around. The show, a resounding success, established Cody as one of the founders of modern-day rodeo and became the preview of the great Wild West shows which were to follow.

For his first Wild West Show, which had its opening performance the following year, Cody gathered together hard-riding cowboys, numerous bucking broncos and saddle horses, stage coaches, and a selection of animals, both domestic and wild. Indians were secured with the approval of the Bureau of Indian Affairs, and a group of Mexican riders and ropers was employed. With "Doc" Carver, the shooting expert, as Cody's partner, such people as Maj. John Burke in charge of advertising, and Maj. Frank North, Jule Keene, Capt. A. H. Bogardus, and Johnny Baker in either staff or arena positions, the show was launched in the Omaha fairground on May 19, 1883. An area considerably larger than two football fields, with seating capacity for twenty-five thousand, was soon needed. By the time the first-year's performance reached Connecticut in July, the *Hartford Courant* had called it the "best open-air show ever seen," and Buffalo Bill had become the star of the cast.

Annie Oakley, or "Little Sure Shot," as she was called by the Sioux leader Sitting Bull, joined the Wild West Show in 1884, shortly after Nate Salsbury supplanted Carver as Cody's partner. Annie, who was christened Phoebe Ann Moses, became the best-known woman in outdoor show business. Buffalo Bill first introduced her as "Little Missie, Miss Annie Oakley," and instructed all the men to welcome and protect her. A fantastic marksman and an accomplished actress with an appealing personality, Annie became a great star of the show, receiving prominent billing and appearing early in all performances.

On parting with Cody she said, "I traveled with him for seventeen years—there were thousands of men in the outfit during that time, Comanches, Cowboys, Arabs, Cossacks, and every kind of person, and the whole time we were one great family

Louis Maurer. *The Great Royal Buffalo Hunt.* 1895. Oil, 34 x 54″

Ned Buntline, Buffalo Bill, Milli Morlacchi, and Texas Jack Omohundro as they appeared on stage in the Eastern theatre circuit, 1872–73

loyal to a man. His words were more than most contracts. Personally I never had a contract with the show after I started. It would have been superfluous."

"Little Missie" was reported to have made a million dollars in her years with the Wild West Show, and an even larger number of friends. Her shooting with either rifle or shotgun, from the arena stand or on horseback, was always exciting and accurate. Her husband, Frank Butler, held a cigarette in his lips, a dime in his fingers, or a playing card in his hand for Annie to shoot—thus giving rise to the expression "an Annie Oakley" to describe a ticket or complimentary pass punched to limit its use.

Sitting Bull admired Annie so much that he adopted her into his tribe as a daughter. Her presence in the Wild West Show persuaded the old medicine chief to sign on with the show himself, and he toured for some months in 1885, leaving with satisfaction and a high regard for *Pahaska* (the Indian name given to Buffalo Bill, which means "long-haired chief").

Other outstanding people in the show were Buck Taylor, King of the Cowboys; Bronco Bill Irving; Antonio Esquivel, champion *vaquero* and horseman; and Johnny Baker, trick shot and protégé of Buffalo Bill. The season of 1885, during which the show appeared before its first million people, netted a handsome profit. The Wild West Show was beginning a twenty-five-year tenure as a major attraction in this country and Europe. Buffalo Bill shooting at glass balls from his galloping horse became a treasured symbol. Before long, Cody dropped his winter appearances on the stage and devoted himself wholly to the Wild West Show.

When Queen Victoria was celebrating the fiftieth year of her reign with a Golden Jubilee in London in 1887, the American contribution to this celebration featured Buffalo Bill's Wild West Show, and great plans were made for the show's first visit beyond the limits of its native land.

Lithograph posters in color featuring Cody and others in the Wild West Show were made for the English tour by A. Hoen & Company of Baltimore. Testimonials by most of the famous officers of the Western army, including Lt. Gen. Philip Sheridan, attesting to the unimpeachable character and valuable services performed by Buffalo Bill, were prepared as introductions to the British people. The title of Colonel, which had been conferred on Cody with his appointment on March 8, 1887, as aide-de-camp in the National Guard by the governor of Nebraska, was seized upon by the English press, and used by Buffalo Bill from that time forward.

The Wild West Cowboy Band played the old military favorite "The Girl I Left Behind Me" as the liner *State of Nebraska* left her New York pier on March 31. Well over two hundred performers of many nationalities were aboard, as well as 180 horses, 18 buffalo, 10 mules, several Texas longhorn steers, and a number of elk and deer. After a very stormy crossing, during which many of the Indian contingent were sure they would not survive, an extravagant welcome was extended by English officials on April 16, and the show moved in three trains to its London location at Earl's Court.

On May 11 a special performance was given for Queen Victoria, during which the monarch and her staff saluted the American flag—the first time it had been so honored by a British sovereign. The show was so well received that a second command presentation was given in June for the queen and her Jubilee guests. It was one of

James Butler "Wild Bill" Hickok. Appeared on the stage with Cody, 1874.

the greatest and most imposing assemblies of European royalty ever brought together. Kings, queens, and nearly twenty members of various European royal families were in attendance. Four kings and the Prince of Wales rode in the Deadwood stage coach during a simulated Indian attack, making up a real "royal flush," as Colonel Cody, the driver, said later. Royalty, members of Parliament, and key government figures wined and dined the colonel, who was the hero of the London social season—and who performed as gracefully in full dress suit as he had in buckskins.

Two years later found the Wild West Show again on foreign ground, this time in Paris, and the French were equally enthusiastic about the Western milieu portrayed to them. Rosa Bonheur, the world-famous horse painter, spent much of the seven months of the Wild West Show's Paris engagement painting horses and buffalo in its back lots. She completed several paintings, including a depiction of Indians attacking buffalo; her most famous work is undoubtedly the portrait of Col. William F. Cody reproduced in this book. Some years later, when Cody was informed that his home in Nebraska, Welcome Wigwam, was afire, he sent a telegram saying: "Save the Rosa Bonheur and let the flames take the rest."

Possibly it was Cody's association with Rosa Bonheur that stimulated his appreciation of art. Later years found him frequently among artist friends: Frederic Remington, Irving R. Bacon, Ashley D. M. Cooper, H. H. Cross, Charles Schreyvogel, and others from whom he purchased or commissioned paintings. His interest in Western art was perhaps among the earliest in the field. H. Farrington Elwell was given

Scout's Rest Ranch, Cody's home in North Platte, Nebraska

Sitting Bull, the famous Sioux
medicine chief, and Cody, 1885

Annie Oakley wearing some of the
medals she later melted down to
purchase World War I liberty
bonds, c. 1900

Charles Schreyvogel. *The Summit Springs Rescue.*
1908. Oil, 48 x 66''

Frederic Remington. *In the Spotlight.* Oil. 24 x 36"

a job on Cody's famous TE Ranch in Wyoming while still a boy, so that he could study and draw the life of the West.

The bulk of Colonel Cody's imposing collection of Western art eventually found a home in his Irma Hotel in Cody, Wyoming. (The collection came to the Buffalo Bill Memorial Association as a gift on the death of Pearl C. Newell, who had purchased the property and art from the Cody estate.)

In the winter of 1890-91, after a tour of central Europe and Italy, Buffalo Bill

The cowboy band of the Wild West Show
and some of the show's personnel

served for the last time with the army as a guide and scout. At that time, the Ghost Dance cult, a messianic movement whose basic tenets were that dead Indians would come back to life and that white men would disappear, leaving Indian life as it was before their arrival, was spreading among the Plains Indians. Sitting Bull, then living on a Sioux reservation, was one of the cult's apostles, and it was feared that he would use his influence to foment an uprising of all the Indians in the country. At the request of Gen. Nelson A. Miles, commanding general of the army, Cody set out for the Stand-

continued on page 66

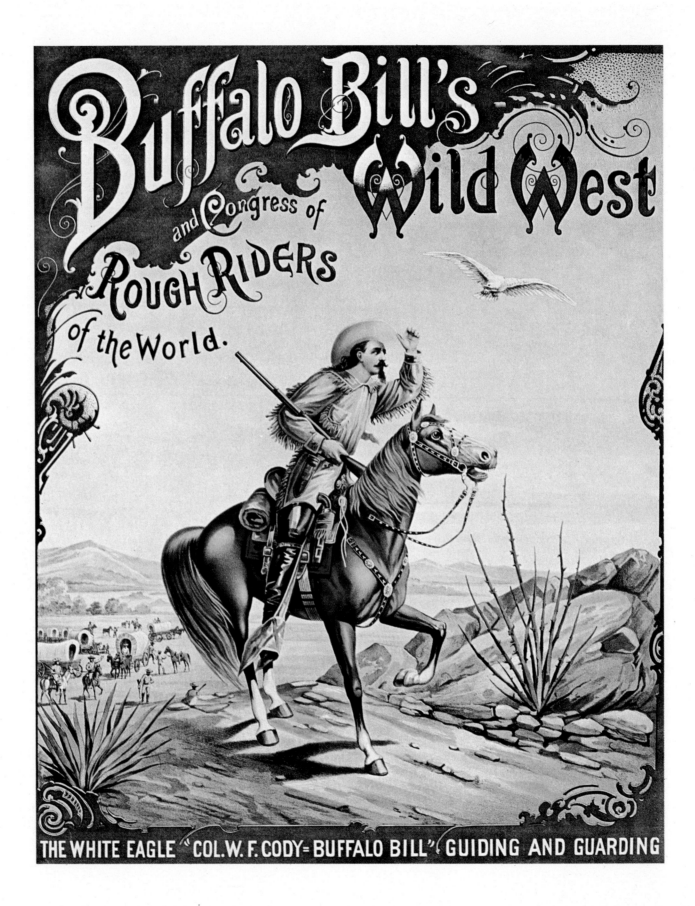

The White Eagle. Poster for the Wild West Show, 24 x 19″. Printed by A. Hoen & Co., Baltimore, c. 1887

The Red Fox. Poster for the Wild
West Show, 24 x 19″. Printed by
A. Hoen & Co., Baltimore, 1887

Poster for Sells-Floto Circus. 1913

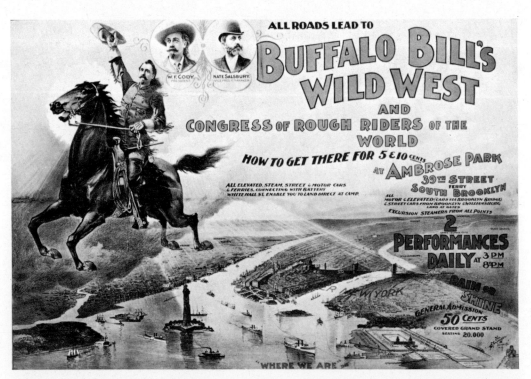

Posters for the Wild West Show

BUFFALO BILL TO THE RESCUE.

Posters for the Wild West Show

The Farewell Shot. Poster, 40 x 26″. Printed by U.S. Lithograph Co., Cincinnati and New York, 1910

Miss Annie Oakley. Poster for the Wild West Show, 28 x 16″. Printed by A. Hoen & Co., Baltimore, 1887

"A Factor of International Amity."
Poster, 36 x 28″. Printed by A. Hoen &
Co., Baltimore, 1887

Poster showing some of the generals of the U.S. Army under whom Cody served, 24 x 34″. Printed by A. Hoen & Co., Baltimore, 1887

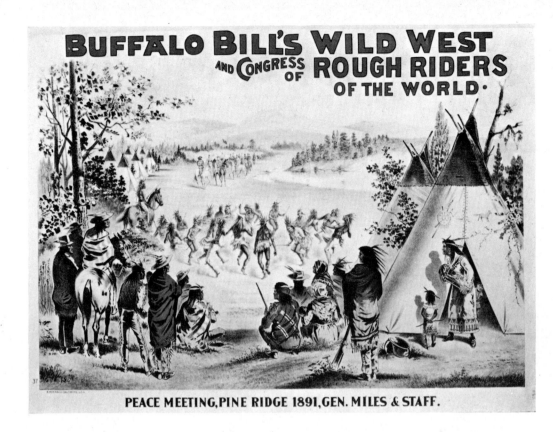

PEACE MEETING, PINE RIDGE 1891, GEN. MILES & STAFF.

COL. W. F. CODY (BUFFALO BILL) A CLOSE CALL.

Posters for the Wild West Show

◄ Irving R. Bacon. *Pals of 1876* (showing Ned Buntline, Cody, and Texas Jack Omohundro). 1904. Oil, 26 x 22″

Robert Lindneux. *First Scalp for Custer.* 1928. Oil, 72 x 168″

Irving R. Bacon. *The Horse Thieves.* 1902. Oil, 18 x 26″

Irving R. Bacon. *The Life I Love.*
1902. Oil, 22 x 34″

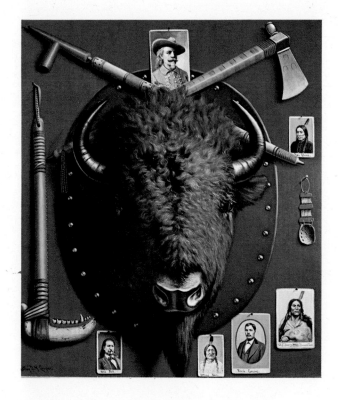

Ashley D. M. Cooper. *The Buffalo Head.* c. 1890.
Oil, 40 x 36″

Philip Ayer Sawyer. *A Congress of
Rough Riders.* 1929. Oil, 5′ 10″ x 9′

Arthur Jule Goodman. *King Edward VII at the Wild West.* 1903. Pastel, 40 x 27"

Lassoing Wild Mustangs. Early poster for the Wild West Show, 28 x 38″. Printed by A. Hoen & Co., Baltimore

Bucking Mustangs. Early poster for the Wild West Show, 28 x 38″. Printed by A. Hoen & Co., Baltimore

ing Rock Agency to contact Sitting Bull and try to convince him not to incite an uprising. When Cody arrived at the agency on November 28, however, the government agent, who felt that the prerogatives of his Indian police were being interfered with, prevented him from proceeding to Sitting Bull's camp. Two weeks later the Indian police seized the chief. His warriors attempted to free him, and Sitting Bull was killed in the skirmish. The army, fearing more trouble, vanquished the Sioux in a final battle at Wounded Knee (December 29), in which Cody did not participate. After serving as adjutant general of the state of Nebraska, Buffalo Bill ceased military activity for the rest of his life, though he tried unsuccessfully to go to Cuba to take part in the Spanish-American War of 1898.

While Cody was involved in military activities, his partner, Nate Salsbury, was in Alsace-Lorraine reorganizing the Wild West Show, and it opened the 1893 season under the title "Buffalo Bill's Wild West and Congress of Rough Riders of the World." Designed to display expert horsemanship from nations all over the world, it was a fast-moving, tightly controlled presentation that appealed greatly to all those who saw it. There were 640 members of the troupe, plus nearly 500 horses, and the whole organization participated in a morning parade and two performances daily, moving at night by railroad to the next location. During the show's tour of Germany, the kaiser's army took an intense interest in Cody's organization, noting in official books all the details of train-loading, tent-pitching, operation of field kitchens, and the like. In 1895 the show was presented in 131 locations within 190 days.

Perhaps the most successful of all the years Buffalo Bill's show operated was 1893, during which it appeared in Chicago at the World's Columbian Exposition. As was true of the exposition, the show set records for attendance that have never been surpassed. Over 700,000 people paid admission to the exposition on Chicago Day, October 9. The Wild West Show performed, to capacity crowds, the program reproduced below:

Irving R. Bacon. *Colonel Cody and General Miles.* 1911. Oil, 32 x 50"

The Wild West Show cast, 1906

OVERTURE, "Star Spangled Banner"
Cowboy Band, Wm. Sweeney, Leader

1. *Grand Review* introducing the Rough Riders of the World and fully Equipped Regular Soldiers of the Armies of America, England, France, Germany, and Russia.

2. *Miss Annie Oakley,* celebrated shot, who will illustrate her dexterity in the use of Firearms.

3. *Horse Race* between a Cowboy, a Cossack, a Mexican, an Arab, and an Indian, on Spanish-Mexican, Bronco, Russian, Indian, and Arabian Horses.

4. *Pony Express,* the Former Pony Post Rider will show how the letters and telegrams of The Republic were distributed across the Immense Continent previous to the Railways and the Telegraph.

5. *Illustrating a Prairie Emigrant Train Crossing The Plains.* Attack by marauding Indians repulsed by "Buffalo Bill" with Scouts and Cowboys. N.B.—The Wagons are the same as used 35 years ago.

Cody with a group of cowboy performers in the Wild West Show, c. 1895

13. *Capture of the Deadwood Mail Coach by the Indians*, which will be rescued by "Buffalo Bill" and his attendant Cowboys. N.B. This is the identical old Deadwood Coach, called the Mail Coach, which is famous on account of having carried the great number of people who lost their lives on the road between Deadwood and Cheyenne 18 years ago. Now the most famed vehicle extant.

14. *Racing between Indian Boys on Bareback Horses.*

15. *Life Customs of the Indians.* Indian Settlement on the Field and "Path."

16. *Col. W. F. Cody* ("Buffalo Bill"), in his Unique Feats of Sharpshooting.

17. *Buffalo Hunt*, as it is in the Far West of North America—"Buffalo Bill" and Indians. The last of the only known Native Herd.

18. *The Battle of the Little Big Horn*, Showing with Historical Accuracy the scene of Custer's Last Charge. [Early in the season the spectacle was: *Attack on a Settler's Cabin*—Capture by the Indians—Rescue by "Buffalo Bill" and the Cowboys.]

19. *Salute*

Conclusion

6. *Group of Syrian and Arabian Horsemen* will illustrate their style of Horsemanship, with native Sports and Pastimes.

7. *Cossacks*, of the Caucasus of Russia, in Feats of Horsemanship, Native Dances, etc.

8. *Johnny Baker*, Celebrated Young American Marksman.

9. *A Group of Mexicans* from Old Mexico, will illustrate the use of The Lasso, and per-form various Feats of Horsemanship.

10. *Racing Between Prairie, Spanish and Indian Girls.*

11. *Cowboy Fun.* Picking Objects from the Ground, Lassoing Wild Horses, Riding the Buckers.

12. *Military Evolutions* by a Company of the Sixth Cavalry of the United States Army; a Company of the First Guard Uhlan Regiment of His Majesty King William II, German Emperor, popularly known as The "Potsdamer Reds"; a Company of French Chasseurs (Chasseurs a Cheval de la Garde République Français); and a Company of the 12th Lancers (Prince of Wales' Regiment) of the British Army.

Buffalo Bill and the cast
of the Wild West Show in
the arena, 1906

Kit Carson Cody, Colonel Cody's only son,
at the age of five, 1876

The Cody's first child, a daughter christened Arta Cody, was born in December 1866 at Leavenworth, Kansas, while her father was scouting for the army. Cody's only son arrived in November 1870 at Fort McPherson, Nebraska; and was named after the famous scout Kit Carson, who was a close friend of Buffalo Bill. A second daughter, Orra Maude, was born at Fort McPherson on August 15, 1872, not long after the great buffalo hunt with the Grand Duke Alexis. The baby of the family, Irma Louise, who later gave her name to a famous hotel in the town of Cody, was born in February 1883 in North Platte, Nebraska, while her father was putting together his first Wild West Show.

Tragedy struck the Cody family in 1876 when little Kit Carson died from scarlet fever in Rochester, New York, where the family lived while Buffalo Bill was on the theater circuit. Shortly after Irma was born, Orra Maude contracted an illness that caused her death. Left with the oldest and youngest daughters, the Codys gave them every advantage, and both grew into beautiful young women with families of their own.

By the 1890s Colonel Cody's Scout's Rest Ranch in Nebraska had become the showplace of the region. With fine fields and good horses and cattle, the operation was a great success under the direction of Cody's brother-in-law Al Goodman. Satisfied with his enterprise but remembering Professor Marsh's description of the Big Horn basin in Wyoming, Buffalo Bill decided to invest in the area named for General Sheridan, just east of the basin. After a year or two, however, he gave up his interests there and crossed the Big Horn Mountains into what is now Park County, Wyoming.

Cody found an untouched, virgin country, with much wildlife and a truly exciting potential. Gathering together some friends and business associates, he set out to develop the area for settlement. He acquired a ranch, naming it the TE Ranch for the large number of TE-branded cattle that he imported from Nebraska. This ranch became his hideaway and rest area when he was not on tour with the Wild West Show. He added the Carter and Rock creek ranches to his property, building all three into a fine stock-raising project and a sprawling place of peace and contentment.

At the same time, he and his friends set about locating a town site, and acquiring water rights and building irrigation canals. A town to be called Shoshone was staked out near Cedar Mountain at the mouth of Shoshone Canyon, just below where the Shoshone River is formed by the junction of the north and south forks. The United States government vetoed the suggested town name of Shoshone, fearing it would be confused with the Shoshoni Indian reservation farther south. While Colonel Cody was in the East with his Wild West Show, his friends, headed by George T. Beck, moved the location of the town site downstream a few miles to a wider area and submitted the name of Cody, which was accepted.

Colonel Cody prevailed on the president of the nearest railroad to build a spur track into the newly formed town and end its isolation from other areas of development. A railroad was especially important to agriculture interests that found the country attractive. He also convinced the federal government to provide funds to build a road from Cody through the east entrance of Yellowstone National Park, the first of our great national parks, established in 1872.

Cody and his wife with their daughters
Arta and Orra, 1882

The TE ranch house, Cody's ranch in Wyoming

A sketch by Frederic Remington done for Irma Cody on the occasion of the opening of the Irma Hotel, November 1902

Near the park entrance in the Shoshone Forest, Buffalo Bill built his big log hunting lodge, Pahaska. Here he entertained royalty from Europe, newspapermen, and friends on great hunts for the big-game animals so abundant in the region. Camp Monaco was established nearby as the headquarters of Prince Albert of Monaco, who hunted extensively in the area. Today Pahaska is a mountain tourist village catering to the numerous automobile travelers to Yellowstone National Park.

In 1902, shortly after the arrival of the railroad in Cody, the construction on the Irma Hotel was completed. The Irma was one of the finest hostelries in a wide area, and today is still the social center of the community. Its opening was the occasion for a gala party attended by many notable people from throughout the United States. Frederic Remington danced with Irma Cody and drew doodles commemorating the evening.

After the incorporation of the town, Buffalo Bill visited an old friend, President Theodore Roosevelt. Roosevelt had borrowed the name "Rough Riders" from the Wild West Show for his troops in the Spanish-American War in Cuba. With the president's help and in cooperation with the newly formed Bureau of Reclamation, the construction of the Shoshone Dam was undertaken in 1904 and completed five years later. The structure was the first of its type, the first built by the Bureau of Reclamation, and the highest in the world at the time. Flood waters were controlled, electric power generated, and the irrigation system stabilized. Many years later a bill changing the name to the Buffalo Bill Dam, in recognition of the part Colonel Cody played in its erection and in the development of the surrounding areas, was passed by Congress and signed by President Truman.

R. Farrington Elwell. *Pahaska Tepee, Buffalo Bill's Hunting Lodge in the Rockies.* 1904. Oil, 40 x 66"

The Buffalo Bill Dam, along the road from Cody to Yellowstone Park

Cody City, as its founders sometimes called it, came into its own during those early years. Irrigation insured the success of agriculture and livestock operations, tourists to Yellowstone increased, and Cody became the heart of the dude ranch country, where Easterners could enjoy a vacation on a real Western ranch. Oil was later discovered in the area, and the economy was thereby further stimulated.

From the end of the 1908 season through that of 1912, Buffalo Bill and Pawnee Bill (Major Gordon Lillie) were partners in Buffalo Bill's Wild West and Pawnee Bill's Far East. It was known among the performers as "the Two Bills' show." The men

The "Two Bills". Poster showing Pawnee Bill (Maj. Gordon Lillie) and Buffalo Bill, 38 x 26". Printed by U.S. Lithograph Co., Cincinnati and New York, 1912

Buffalo Bill with Pawnee, Crow, and Sioux
scouts, 1875

Buffalo Bill Cody, 1907. Photograph, hand-tinted
in 1959 by Adolph Sphor

William F. Cody, founder of
Cody, Wyoming, 1907

Buffalo Bill: Man of Vision, 1905

Cody with his doctor in Glenwood Springs, Colorado,
December 1916. The last photograph of Cody

Buffalo Bill in the lobby of the Irma Hotel, Cody, Wyoming, 1907

Colonel and Mrs. Cody at the Irma Hotel with grandchildren and friends, 1915

worked well together in a successful operation. Colonel Cody had long wished to retire from the rigors of show business, but unproductive investments and heavy commitments kept him active. During this period he advertised a series of "farewell" appearances, hoping each year to be in a position to retire.

Financial troubles with Frederick G. Bonfils and Harry H. Tammen, publishers of the *Denver Post*, caused the partnership between Cody and Lillie to dissolve, resulting in a sale of the assets of the Wild West Show by public auction. Colonel Cody never again was an active owner or manager of an outdoor show, though he appeared with two before his death. He did initiate a venture with the Essanay Film Company of Chicago, and, with the help of the army, made a series of historical films depicting Indian and army battles, Wounded Knee among them.

In 1914 and 1915 Buffalo Bill was the star attraction of the Sells-Floto Circus on long tours of one-day stands. The 101 Ranch Show featured him in 1916, and he left at the end of that season in a state of near exhaustion.

After a brief visit to Cody and his beloved TE Ranch, he caught a severe cold which developed into pneumonia with complications. He went to the medical baths in Glenwood Springs, Colorado, to recuperate. There he suffered a nervous collapse and was removed to his sister's home in Denver, where he died on January 10, 1917.

This country and the world mourned his death with deep sorrow. Tributes and resolutions came to his family in uncountable numbers from all classes of people. As the years pass, his image and deeds are undiminished, and he continues to fill his place as part of our heritage. Perhaps he is best loved, remembered, and memorialized by the people of Cody, Wyoming, who really knew him.

Buffalo Bill bowing at the conclusion of a Wild West Show performance close to the end of his career, 1913

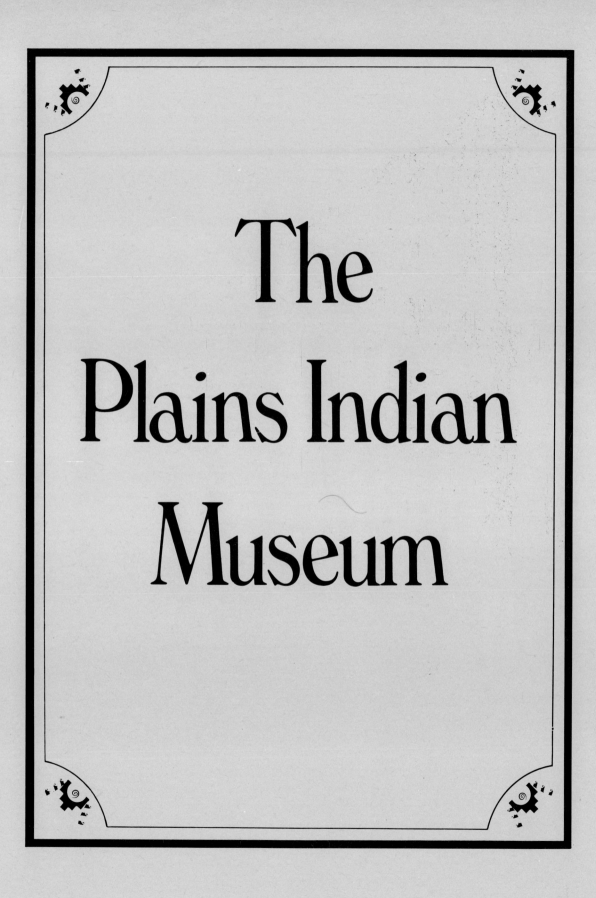

The
Plains Indian
Museum

Sacred Thunder medicine pipe. Blackfoot. c. 1870 or earlier

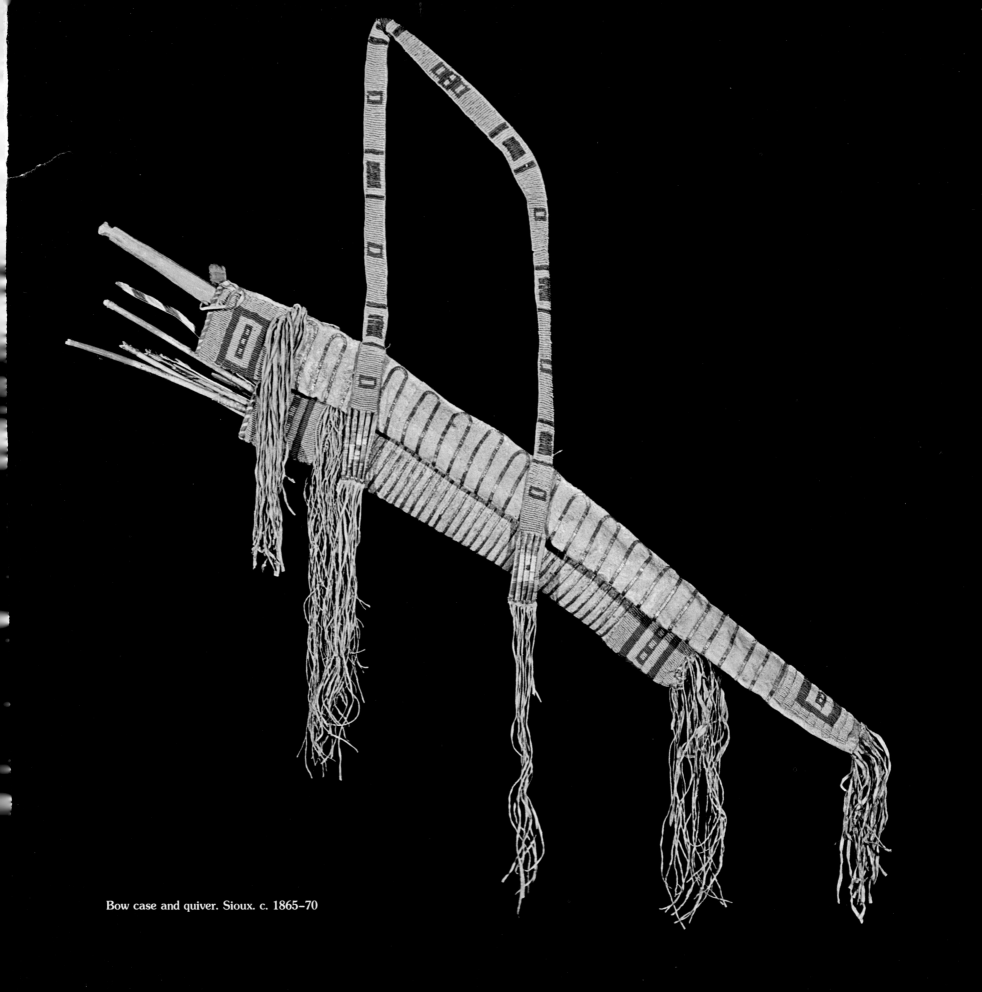

Bow case and quiver. Sioux. c. 1865–70

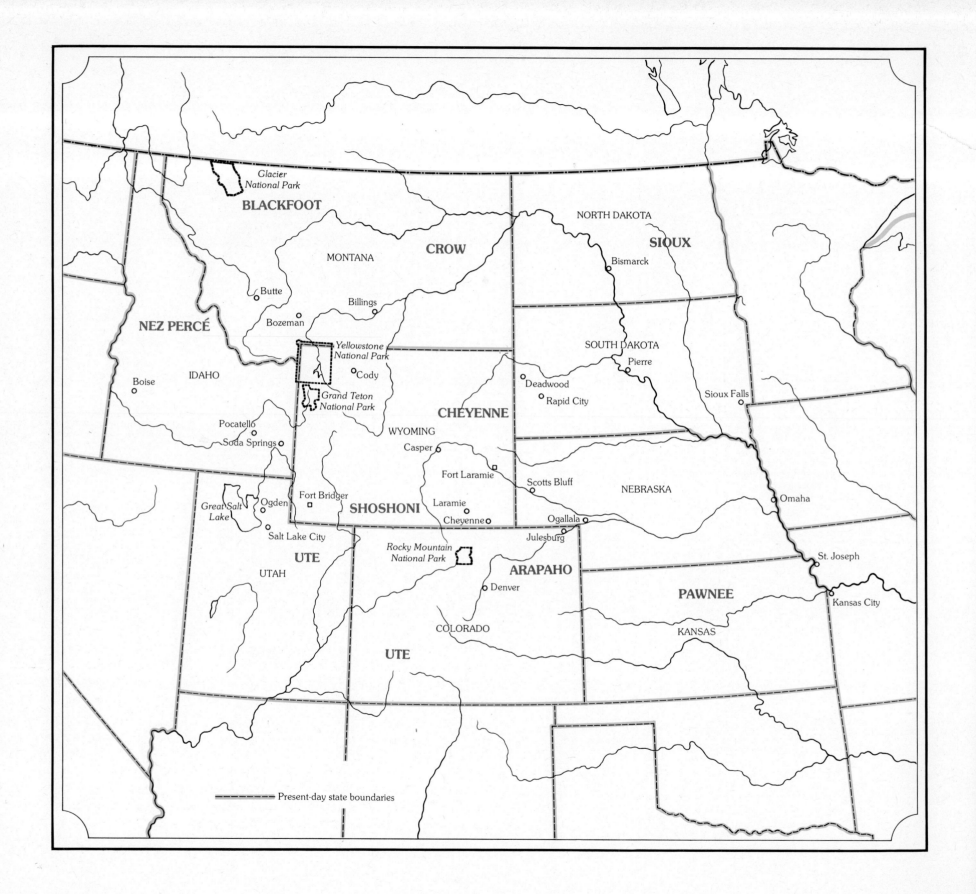

Glacier
National Park

BLACKFOOT

NORTH DAKOTA

CROW

SIOUX

MONTANA

Bismarck

Butte

Billings

Bozeman

NEZ PERCÉ

Yellowstone
National Park

SOUTH DAKOTA

Pierre

Cody

IDAHO

Deadwood

Boise

Grand Teton
National Park

Rapid City

Sioux Falls

CHEYENNE

Pocatello

WYOMING

Soda Springs

Casper

Fort Laramie

Scotts Bluff

NEBRASKA

Laramie

Omaha

Great Salt
Lake

Ogden

Fort Bridger

SHOSHONI

Cheyenne

Ogallala

Salt Lake City

Julesburg

St. Joseph

UTE

Rocky Mountain
National Park

ARAPAHO

UTAH

Denver

Kansas City

PAWNEE

COLORADO

KANSAS

UTE

——— Present-day state boundaries

THOUSANDS of years ago, the first small band of Stone Age people wandered onto the North American continent. Whether these nomadic hunters were pursuing animals for food, or were pursued by enemies, we do not know, but we do know that they migrated from northeastern Asia, crossing the Bering Strait over a dry land bridge (exposed when the sea level fell during the last stage of the Ice Age) which once existed between Siberia and Alaska. Over many thousands of years, the inhabitants of the New World wandered from Alaska to the tip of the South American continent and from the Pacific to the Atlantic Oceans. Latecomers, such as the Aleuts and the Eskimos, made open-water crossings in boats from Asia, traveling through the Aleutian Islands to the Alaskan coast and settling throughout the Arctic.

The Indians of the Americas have been divided into twenty-two different culture areas; they spoke over two thousand different languages. What the total population was in the New World at the time of the white man's arrival is a matter of speculation. However, the generally accepted figure for North America is about 1,150,000, with about 850,000 living within the present boundaries of the continental United States.

On October 12, 1492, Christopher Columbus anchored his ships in Long Bay at Guanahani Island. Going ashore, he claimed the island for the Catholic sovereigns of Spain, naming it San Salvador. (It is also known as Watling Island.) The peaceful natives who witnessed this ceremony believed that the ships and the crew had descended from the sky. These were the Taino people, of the Arawakan stock; their ancestors had navigated to San Salvador and other nearby islands from the mainland of South America.

Believing that he had reached the East Indies, Columbus gave the natives of the New World the misnomer *Indios,* "Indians." Some years later, in 1507, Martin Waldsee-müller, a German geographer, read an account by the Italian navigator Amerigo Vespucci of a voyage to South America. On the basis of this account. Waldseemuller mistakenly decided that Vespucci had discovered the New World, and suggested that it be called "America."

In 1899 Maj. John Wesley Powell, Director of the Bureau of Ethnology of the Smithsonian Institution, urged that the term "American Indian" be changed to "Amerind." While "Amerind" sometimes appears in scientific and popular literature, the term "Indian" has prevailed. The tribal names that the Indians gave themselves commonly meant "the People"; the names by which the various tribes are known today were given to them by other neighboring tribes or by white men.

Typical Plains Indians were first encountered in 1541 by the Spanish explorer Francisco Coronado and his men. After horses were acquired in 1598 from the Spanish settlements in what is now New Mexico and spread slowly northward, the Plains Indian culture as we think of it began to emerge. This equestrian culture was at its zenith about the time of the Lewis and Clark expedition (1804–6). Although contact with white men became more frequent in the next few years, the Plains civilization was still unspoiled when artists such as George Catlin and Karl Bodmer visited the tribes on the Upper Missouri River in the early 1830s.

The Plains Indian people ranged over a geographical area spreading from the Mississippi River and northern Texas to the Rocky Mountains and adjacent parts of Canada. They can be divided into two distinct subcultures.

Nomadic tribes displayed the most typical cultural characteristics of the Plains people. These were hunting people whose principal source of food, clothing, and shelter was the buffalo. They lived in portable *tipis* (from the Siouan *ti,* "to dwell," plus *pi,* "used for"), conical frameworks of poles covered with dressed buffalo skins. Included in this group were the Arapaho, Assiniboin, Blackfeet, Cheyenne, Comanche, Crow, Gros Ventre, Kiowa, and Teton Sioux.

Seminomadic tribes spent part of the year living in permanent villages consisting of circular earth- or grass-covered lodges and practiced some agriculture. Periodically they wandered into the buffalo country for food, during which time they lived in tipis. These tribes included the Arikara, Hidatsa, Iowa, Kansa, Mandan, Missouri, Omaha, Osage, Oto, Pawnee, Ponca, and Wichita.

There were also a number of marginal and outlying tribes which had some traits typical of the Plains culture (for example, some of them hunted buffalo) but also shared certain distinctive subcultural traits of their own. These tribes included the Bannock,

Caddo, Flathead, Jicarilla Apache, Kiowa Apache, Kutenai, Nez Percé, Plains Cree, Plains Ojibwa, Quapaw, Santee Sioux, Yankton Sioux, Sarsi, Spokane, Ute, and the Wind River Shoshoni.

Sign language, which utilized descriptive hand gestures to convey ideas, provided a means of communication between tribes who were unfamiliar with one another's dialect of speech.

The Plains people were skilled in the use of stone and bone tools and of weapons adapted for hunting the buffalo and other large game. They transported their firewood, meat, and personal possessions on a *travois,* an **A**-shaped frame consisting of two poles. Originally, dogs were used to pull the *travois;* later it was adapted for horses as well. The introduction of the horse revolutionized the culture of the Plains Indians. In addition to their value as pack animals, horses were also used in combat and on buffalo hunts.

The buffalo was the most important and sacred animal in the Plains Indian culture. For the tribal summer buffalo hunt, scattered bands gathered together, erecting their tipis at designated places in the camp circle. A deeply religious people, the Indians prayed to the supernatural powers to guide the herds near their camp, thus ensuring the success of the hunt. Individual hunting was forbidden by strict regulations and was severely punished, since a lone hunter might scatter a buffalo herd, causing hardship for the entire tribe. The most common method of buffalo hunting was the "surround." Mounted hunters armed with lances, short bows (approximately three feet in length, for easy handling on horseback), and, later, firearms, surrounded the herd; getting the animals to bunch up and mill around in a circle, the hunters brought them down one by one. Another method of hunting on horseback, one which was less dangerous and probably more efficient than the surround, was the chase: the hunters rode alongside the running herd, killing buffalo at point-blank range. Identification marks on a hunter's arrows showed which animals he had killed. If several arrows with different markings were found in one buffalo, the animal was divided proportionately among the hunters. After the kill, women arrived with the pack animals and assisted with the butchering.

The buffalo provided all the necessities of life for the Plains tribes, and these ingenious people devised more than one hundred different uses for the animal. In addition to food, the buffalo furnished winter robes, moccasins, headdresses, and other types of clothing. Hides served as lodge covers, doors, and linings for tipis; hair was used as stuffing for pad-saddles or twisted to make ropes; horns were fashioned into spoons, cups and ladles; rawhide was employed in making shields, *parfleches,* and horse gear; sinew was used for bow strings and thread; the gall was made into yellow paint for ornamental use; the bladder could be used as a container; dried buffalo dung served as fuel for the fires that warmed the Indians' tipis; bones were made into tools and children's sleds. The buffalo skull was an exceptionally important totem which was revered in daily life and used in religious ceremonies.

Plains Indian families were close-knit, with the masculine and feminine roles clearly defined. Men were the hunters, providers, and protectors, engaging in tribal leadership, military organizations, and warfare. Women tanned hides, made clothing, prepared food, and performed the other daily chores of camp life; they also took part in certain organizations and craft guilds. Children were carefree, but were taught to obey and respect their elders. As the children grew older, they were instructed by their parents in their future responsibilities. While girls learned homemaking and crafts from their mothers, boys were taught by their fathers to make weapons and hunt game. Courtship and marriage was encouraged after a young man had earned war honors and had made the proper exchange of gifts with the prospective bride's family. Elderly people were respected and honored for their age and wisdom.

Every facet of the Plains Indians' culture was influenced by their religious beliefs. The Sun Dance was one of their most important and distinctive religious tribal ceremonies. The ceremony was given by an individual in fulfillment of a vow he had made in a time of extreme danger or illness. It took place during the summer, usually in July, but sometimes in August, and generally lasted for eight days, including four preliminary days of preparations and four days of dancing. The ceremony had variations among the different tribes, but generally the ritual proceeded as follows: A tree considered worthy to serve as the sacred pole for the circular Sun Dance lodge was selected. The lodge was then erected, and an area for an altar was cleared within it; a painted buffalo skull was placed at the center of this cleared space. The initiates danced around the sacred pole, gazing steadily at the sacred medicine bundle at its top. Voluntary self-torture was sometimes a part of the ceremony; wooden skewers on ropes which led to the top of the Sun Dance pole were inserted in the dancers' chests through cuts in the pectoral muscles; the initiates, blowing on whistles, struggled backward until the skewers were torn from their bodies.

For the Indians, this was a sacred and joyful occasion. It was a time of thanksgiving because the dancers had willingly suffered to renew the holy blessings for all the people. Among the tribes who celebrated the Sun Dance ceremony were the Arapaho, Arikara, Assiniboin, Blackfeet, Cheyenne, Crow, Gros Ventre, Hidatsa, Kiowa, Plains Cree, Plains Ojibwa, Ponca, Sarsi, Sioux, Ute, and Wind River Shoshoni.

Summer was the only season of the year when the scattered bands of a tribe gathered together in one large camp. After the conclusion of the Sun Dance ceremony, the various bands again went their separate ways for the fall hunt. In the fall, in addition to hunting buffalo, the Indians collected berries and prepared food for storage, continuing these activities until the weather forced them to stop. They camped for the winter, usually in a timbered river valley which provided some protection from the wind and snow. Such valleys offered water, firewood, grass for the horses, and proximity to buffalo and other game. (The buffalo did not migrate south for the winter—a widespread but erroneous belief—but remained in the Plains, making treks into wooded areas which provided shelter from blizzards.) Since the hair of the buffalo was thicker and longer during the winter months, the heaviest robes were obtained during this season. In early spring, the buffalo began to move away from the Indians' winter camps, and, with their meat supply dwindling, the Indians moved too. Spring kept the Indians busy hunting, collecting plants for food, and making and repairing personal belongings for the oncoming warm weather. Before long, it would again be time for the summer tribal gathering.

Intertribal warfare was a deadly game of bravado with the Plains Indians. Small parties of warriors raided enemy camps to steal or to gain revenge. The winning of war honors, or *coups,* on the battlefield was a way of earning glory and social prestige.

Although the Indians resisted the penetration of the Spanish, French, English, Mexicans, and Americans into the Plains for two-and-a-half centuries, they were not consistently hostile toward the whites during the early years of westward expansion. Large-scale warfare did not erupt on the Plains until the white men's constant harassment threatened to end the Indians' nomadic way of life forever.

After the Lewis and Clark Expedition in 1804–6, the new Western frontier attracted adventurous trappers and traders. These rugged mountain men lived among the various tribes and often married Indian women. They brought with them a variety of trade items, including glass beads, cloths, blankets, metal adzes, and knives. These marvelous goods, the supply of which was always shorter than the demand, had a great impact on Plains culture.

In the 1840s, the Indians were becoming increasingly alarmed at the growing numbers of trespassers crossing their sacred hunting grounds. But the tide of settlers continued to push westward across the Mississippi, founding more towns, forts, and homesteads; and by mid-century the culture of the Plains Indians had begun to disappear. The whites, greedy for the Indians' land, broke a succession of treaties and promises. Treaties were also occasionally broken by Indians who were distrustful of the white men's motives. Eventually, conflicts erupted.

The desperate Indian wars that swept across the Plains began with an uprising of the Santee Sioux on a quiet Sunday—August 17, 1862—near New Ulm, Minnesota. Years of bloody conflict followed, with horrible atrocities committed by both Indians and whites.

By the late nineteenth century, the whites had prevailed, and most of the Plains people were living on government reservations.

Of all those who came to the West—explorers, mountain men, pioneers, miners, soldiers, cowboys, homesteaders—none had a more devastating effect on the culture of the Plains Indians than the white buffalo hunters. Between 1871 and 1883, the hidemen engaged in a wanton slaughter of the animals, virtually wiping them out. Estimates of the total number of buffalo once living on the Plains range from thirty to seventy-five million. Surveys show that by 1889 slightly more than five hundred buffalo remained in the entire United States, with only eighty-five on the open range.

Confined to government reservations, their nomadic way of life destroyed, the Indians believed that the buffalo had disappeared as a punishment for their wrongdoings. They prayed to the supernatural powers for the return of the herds. In 1888 the Ghost Dance religion, which had appeared in an early form in 1870, reemerged on the Plains. Wovoka, a Paiute Indian, became the leader of the movement. He taught his followers to perform a dance which he said would result in the disappearance of the whites, the reuniting of Indians with their dead, and the return of the Buffalo, making the land rich and the people happy forever. During the next two years, armed insurrection against the white men broke out. The Sioux followers of the cult began to wear special shirts which they believed were impervious to bullets. But the insurrection was short-lived. The Ghost Dance came to an end on December 29, 1890, with the final defeat of the Indians at Wounded Knee, on the frozen, snow-covered plains of South Dakota.

Buffalo Bill's Wild West Show was the most exciting form of entertainment in its day. All over the world, people were thrilled by the cowboys, Mexican *vaqueros*, bucking horses, and attacking, war-bonneted Indians.

For those Indians who were fortunate enough to be selected, the Wild West Show meant employment and a chance to observe the white man's ways throughout the country. It also provided a means of escaping from the hated government reservations. There was more self-respect to be gained by participating in sham battles than by rotting on a patch of barren ground.

Although Buffalo Bill had fought Indians in the years before his show, those in the troupe looked upon Cody as a friend who treated them with respect and dignity. Many prominent Indians, including the Sioux leaders Red Cloud, American Horse, and Sitting Bull, appeared in the show on different occasions.

As far as Buffalo Bill was concerned, his word to the Indians was a bond. He knew that they would have nothing but contempt for a liar, and he made sure his other employees were aware of this fact.

The Indians in the show were well-treated. They received pay, plenty to eat, and were allowed to come and go like other employees. Their general situation was much better than that of Indians confined to reservations.

Knowing that Buffalo Bill was concerned for their well-being, the Indians in his show often presented him with gifts as tokens of their friendship. He acquired over the years a great number of costumes and artifacts, which are now housed in the Plains Indian Museum of the Buffalo Bill Historical Center.

The Plains Indian material originally collected by Buffalo Bill, and additional material acquired from other donors, is important for both ethnological and historical reasons. We are proud to be the custodians of these reminders of the venerable traditions of the Plains Indians.

The articles in the museum's exhibits reflect the everyday life of the Plains Indians as well as ceremonial practices, religion, and warfare. Elegant costumes for men, women, and children are represented. The arts and crafts illustrate distinctive tribal styles of construction and decoration. In addition, a gradual evolution of designs and materials between the early 1800s and the reservation period is demonstrated.

Among the most historic items in the Plains Indian Museum are ceremonial costumes belonging to the Sioux leaders Red Cloud and American Horse, the largest and most important collection of Sitting Bull's personal possessions, and a number of items owned by Chief Joseph of the Nez Percé.

It is our desire to preserve all facets of the Plains Indian culture and to reflect in our displays the honor and dignity of these people.

As the distinguished artist-ethnologist Paul Dyck has stated: "The Indians of the West left a heritage of courage, beauty, and philosophy which can inspire and enrich the world."

Arikara shirt   The shirt shown at left is made of tanned deer hide and decorated with dyed porcupine quillwork on buffalo-hide strips. It is trimmed with ermine and fringe. The bottom of the shirt is left untrimmed in the old style, with legs that hang down on each side of the wearer.

Blackfoot medicine man's ceremonial costume   The fur hat on the manikin is made from the skin of a fisher, a rare animal in many areas. The "wings" symbol in front is cloth, overlaid with strings of amber beads. On both sides of the hat are personal medicines (not visible in the photograph): on the left, a fully beaded blue horse design, and on the right, wings from a redwing blackbird. On the back of the hat are two fishers' feet, a beaded awl case, a group of hawk feathers, an entire weasel skin, and several strips of caribou hide.

The small necklace consists of white stone beads interspersed with Venetian polychrome beads and with four antelope horns. A small beaded medicine pouch is in the center, and attached to it are four small pieces of abalone shell, two light-blue, opaque, globular beads, three tails of ermine, and a weasel tail. The large necklace is strung with red mescal seeds; tied to it is a beaver-foot pendant.

Both the beaded caribou-hide shirts and the beaded leggings of wool trade cloth are decorated with ermine skins.

The belt, a trade item, is made of heavy commercial leather and is fastened in back with a serpent-design clasp. The beadwork serves a decorative function.

The beaded moccasins, although of Cheyenne origin, were collected with the costume; they were perhaps a gift of friendship, or the man's wife may have been a Cheyenne.

Suspended from the manikin's hand is a large black-footed weasel decorated with bells and strips of ermine skin—a medicine of the Crow Tobacco Society.

Man's shirt. Arikara. c. 1880

Crow ceremonial costume   The very old buffalo-horn headdress, made of elk skin, extended slightly below the shoulders of the wearer. Attached in back are eighteen bald-eagle feathers, and laced to the front is a green wool forehead band, with the ends hanging down pendant fashion. On each side of the headpiece is a group of seven hawk feathers.

Both the dress coat and the leggings are made of smoked, yellow-ochre-dyed buckskin beaded with the ancient "lotus-flower" design. The coat, which is European in style, is trimmed with beaver fur, fringed, and decorated with red-ochre-dyed "scalp-locks" of horsehair.

The moccasins are of the old-style soft-soled pattern, with the seam on the outside of the foot and up the center of the heel; the instep is fully beaded.

The manikins are displayed standing on a Navajo rug from the area of Tuba City, Arizona. A Cheyenne "dew-cloth" tipi lining was used for the background. Every squaw was required to decorate thirty dew cloths in her lifetime to prove that she was a "good woman."

96

Front and rear views of Blackfoot medicine man's ceremonial costume, c. 1870 *(figure at left in both plates)* and Crow ceremonial costume, c. 1860–70 (right)

Blanket capote. Blackfoot. c. 1875

Man's shirt and feathered
headdress. Gros Ventre. c. 1860-70

Blackfoot blanket capote   A popular trade item with the Indians was the wool "point blanket." Point blankets were introduced into the field in the spring of 1780 by the British Hudson's Bay Company, which had been supplying regular blankets to the Indians since 1681. The "points" and "half points" refer to black lines (about four inches and two inches long, respectively) which indicated the weight, quality, and durability of the blanket. A three-point blanket weighed three pounds and was of better quality than one marked with two and a half points; thus, the more points, the heavier the wool. The blankets came in a variety of colors, including scarlet, empire blue, green, grey, camel, and white. Point blankets were made in private homes until 1866, when mills took over the manufacturing operation.

Blankets, being lighter and less cumbersome to wear, eventually became more common than the traditional fur robes. They also served as beds and bed-covers and were used for many other utilitarian purposes, as well as in ceremonies celebrating courtships, weddings, and other such events. As furs grew more scarce, the demand for blankets increased, making them a particularly valuable item; they were used for barter and made impressive gifts.

Blankets were sometimes made by the Northern Plains tribes into articles of clothing such as leggings and coats. French trappers in the Canadian wilderness gave blanket coats the name *capote*, a military term meaning "a long, hooded overcoat." (Coats made of fur were called *parkas*, a word in the Aleut dialect of the Eskimo language.) *Capotes* were commonly made from the Hudson's Bay Company point blankets. While *capotes* were made in a variety of colors, as blanket leggings were, there was a definite preference for white blankets with black or colored stripes, perhaps because these provided some camouflage for the wearer while he was hunting in a snow-covered area. The *capote* was usually worn with a belt or sash to keep it closed for extra warmth.

The exceptionally fine Blackfoot *capote* at left was made from a three-point Hudson's Bay Company blanket. The body of the *capote* is in one piece, with separate pieces for the hood and sleeves. The hood is fringed and has a tassel hanging from the tip in back; the face opening is bound around the edge with red wool. The shoulders are decorated with beadwork and grizzly-bear claws.

Displayed above the manikin is a pair of Penobscot snowshoes.

Gros Ventre shirt and feathered headdress   The shirt at left was made from a wool trade blanket with an undyed edge. Its beaded shoulder and sleeve strips are trimmed with fringe. Attached to the shoulders are colored ribbons and hawk feathers.

The headdress is made from the tail feathers of the male bald eagle.

Blackfoot shirt and leggings   Frederic Remington, artist and illustrator of the Old West, collected a great deal of Indian paraphernalia on his various trips to the frontier be-

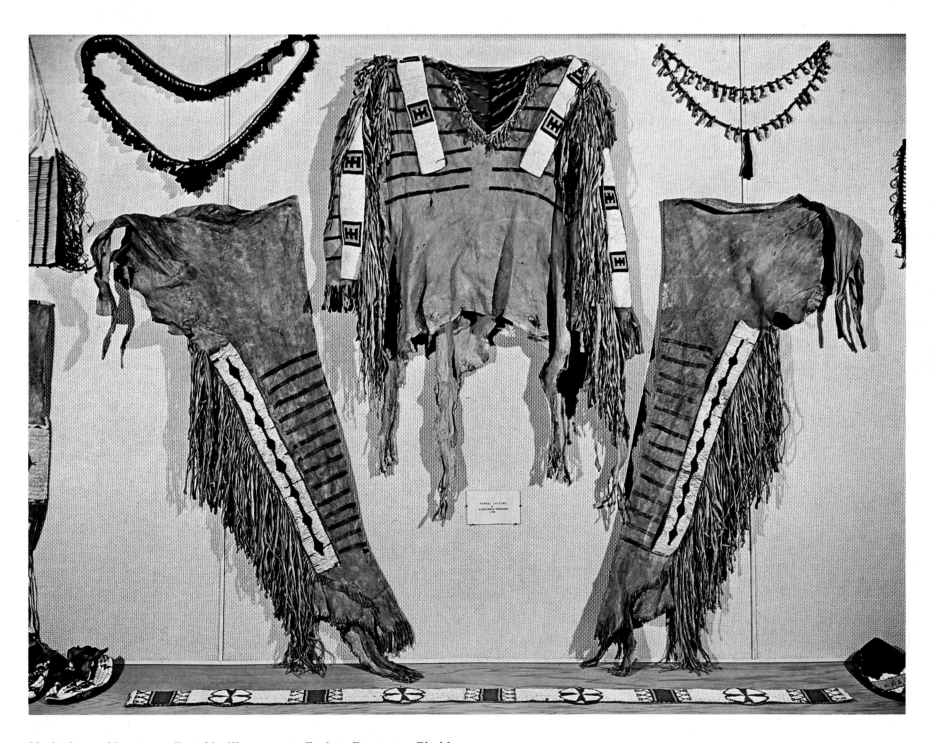

Man's shirt and leggings collected by Western artist Frederic Remington. Blackfoot.
c. 1850

tween 1880 and 1907. The articles illustrated on page 99 were among the contents of Remington's studio at Ridgefield, Connecticut, at the time of his death. Remington had studied them meticulously, using them for details in his pictures.

The deerskin shirt and leggings, which belonged to a member of the Blackfoot tribe, were made about 1850. Both articles are decorated with black stripes of paint and strips of seed beads and are trimmed with fringe. The fringed V-neck of the shirt has a triangular inset of wool trade cloth, half red, half blue. Five narrow rows of diagonal beadwork converge at the center of the inset. The shirt was dyed with yellow ochre, and the bottom was left untrimmed in the old style.

On the left of the shirt is a chipped "dewclaw" (deer-hoof) dance bandolier. On the right is a necklace of teeth interspersed with tin cones; a pendant of buckskin thongs with tin-cone danglers is attached.

Man's shirt. Gros Ventre. 1870

Gros Ventre Shirt   The shirt illustrated at left is made of smoke-tanned deer hide, decorated with dyed porcupine quillwork, and trimmed with ermine and fringe. An extra piece of hide was sewn to the bottom of the shirt to make the sides even.

Crow shirt and tomahawk   Sometime prior to 1805, the Crow Indians became among the first of the Northern Plains tribes to obtain glass trade beads. However, beadwork was of secondary importance to porcupine quillwork until the early 1830s. From this time on, beads were used more prominently, and by the early 1850s they had largely taken the place of quills. Between 1850 and 1890, the Crows developed a highly distinctive style of beaded decoration which gradually replaced quillwork altogether.

The two examples at right illustrate common characteristics of Crow beadwork. The deerskin shirt has an appliquéd neck panel of red wool-flannel trade cloth which is decorated with four narrow horizontal rows of beadwork and a narrow border of white beads. The beaded shoulder strips are divided into a series of blocks, utilizing striped bands of different colors, squares, and solid-colored panels with contrasting borders. The space between the shoulder strip and the neck opening has a narrow beaded band with isosceles triangles touching the center of each side. The shirt is trimmed with ermine skins and scalplocks.

The pipe tomahawk (called "smoak tomahawk" by the English) was a popular trade item in many regions of the United States. The tomahawks of the Plains Indians were frequently decorated with colorful ornaments or personal medicines.

The decorations on the tomahawk make it particularly picturesque. The haft (handle) is partially covered with ochre-dyed moose hide which is fringed on each end and bound to the haft with a buckskin thong. The beaded trade-cloth pendant (similar to those found on the pommels of women's saddles) has its principal design elements outlined with white beads in single lines and is trimmed with fringe. The fore-end projection is decorated with beadwork, ermine, and dyed deer-tail hair.

100

Crow man's shirt with characteristic beadwork, c. 1870, and Crow tomahawk, c. 1870

Nez Percé boy's shirt Children's dress costumes were made in the same basic style as those of adults and often were as colorfully decorated.

Considering the amount of work involved, and how soon the garment would be outgrown, this early example of a little boy's shirt (left) was obviously a labor of love. The block-pattern beadwork of the Nez Percé (with outlines of white beads) undoubtedly reflects their contacts with the Crows.

Boy's shirt. Nez Percé. c. 1860–70

Pawnee Arikara scalp shirt The use of the man's shirt is a comparatively recent development among the Plains Indians; there were probably very few such shirts in existence before 1800. During the early nineteenth century, there was still an absence of shirts among many tribes; in those tribes which did possess them they were worn only by a few distinguished individuals on important ceremonial occasions. Gradually more tribes adopted the shirt, and outstanding examples were depicted by such artists as George Catlin and Karl Bodmer during their journeys among the Indians in the 1830s. After 1850, when the old way of life had started to disappear, the use of the shirt became widespread. Shirts made before 1850 are now extremely rare, a fact which makes them of particular artistic, ethnological, and historical value.

The garment shown at right is one of the oldest and finest scalp shirts in existence. Although possibly of Sioux origin, it is believed to have been worn by Chief Sukhutet of the Pawnee Arikara. It is made from two deerskins in the poncho style, with the natural contour of the hide left untrimmed. The body of the shirt is dyed with two different ochre pigments and trimmed with quill-wrapped scalplocks of human hair. The wool trade-cloth trim on the neck opening and the seed-beaded shoulder and sleeve strips may have been added at a later date.

Sioux ceremonial costume worn by American Horse American Horse was a famous Oglala Sioux chieftain, warrior, and tribal spokesman who fought for better treatment of his people.

In 1886 American Horse and Red Cloud appeared with Buffalo Bill Cody in his Wild West Show at New York's Madison Square Garden. Many prominent Indians, including Sitting Bull of the Hunkpapa Sioux and Chief Joseph of the Nez Percé, appeared in the show throughout the years, and looked upon Cody as a friend who treated them with respect and dignity.

The fine costume shown on pages 104–5 was worn by American Horse. It was presented to Buffalo Bill in 1886, as a token of friendship.

Sioux ceremonial costume worn by Red Cloud Red Cloud (1822–1909) was one of the most famous and powerful chiefs of the Oglala Teton Sioux. Although he had

Scalp shirt worn by Chief Sukhutet. Pawnee Arikara. c. 1800–1810

no hereditary claim to chiefdom, he became the principal leader of the largest band of the Sioux nation through his integrity and achievements. He was a fearless warrior and shrewd military tactician as well as a skilled diplomat and eloquent orator.

The elegant ceremonial costume shown here was worn by Red Cloud. The garment was a mark of distinction among the Sioux people. The double-trail war bonnet, made from the tail feathers of the male bald eagle, shows Red Cloud's prowess as a warrior. It is decorated with eighty-six feathers, each of which represents a deed of valor performed against an enemy in battle. Both the shirt and the leggings, which have been painted, are made of deerskin. The moccasins are decorated with seed beads and feature a thunderbird design.

The distinctively painted shirt, one of the finest in existence, has both ethnological and historical significance. It signified membership in the *Ogle Tanka'un,* or "Shirt Wearers," an elite group of men in the chief's society of the Oglala Sioux. The seven older members of the society, the *Wicasa Itacans,* appointed four young men to this position. Chosen for their courage, integrity, wisdom, compassion, and generosity, the Shirt Wearers were men above reproach who served as tribal counselors dedicated to the welfare of the people. They were appointed for life, but could resign at any time. If a Shirt Wearer failed to act in the interests of the people, he was unshirted, and deprived of his status.

The counselors' special shirts were usually blue and yellow or red and yellow, and had sleeves fringed with scalplocks. The blue-and-yellow colors of the Red Cloud shirt represent the supernatural powers of the universe. The quill-wrapped scalplock fringes represent deeds of warfare, and the people of the tribe. The yellow-dyed scalplocks, of horsehair, symbolize the capture of an enemy's horse.

Some controversy exists about whether or not Red Cloud was actually a Shirt Wearer. According to George E. Hyde, author of *Red Cloud's Folk,* Red Cloud was so honored by 1865. However, Mari Sandoz, author of *Crazy Horse,* writes that Red Cloud was not a Shirt Wearer at that time. Her information was based on the accounts of William Garnett, American Horse, and He Dog (Red Cloud's nephew), all of whom were present at investment ceremonies that year, the latter as initiates. It is possible, however, that Red Cloud was appointed a Shirt Wearer at a later date, perhaps replacing a member of the group who had resigned or had been killed in battle.

On behalf of the Sioux people, Red Cloud made eight official peace crusades to Washington, D. C., between 1870 and 1897. In 1875 and 1877, the Oglala leaders American Horse and Little Wound were part of his delegation. A photograph of the delegation taken in 1877 shows Little Wound wearing the Red Cloud shirt. He is seated beside Red Cloud, who is dressed in white man's clothes. Individual photographs of the three leaders taken during the same period, however, show each of them wearing the shirt. Considering the importance of the Shirt Wearers, and their sacred regard for the special medicinal powers of their shirts, one of the three men may have been required to wear the garment at all public appearances during their visit in Washington. The one thing that can be said with certainty is that the shirt was worn by three distinguished Oglala Sioux leaders.

Sioux ceremonial costumes worn c. 1860–70 by Red Cloud (left) and American Horse (right). Front views on opposite page

Man's shirt worn by Joseph White Coyote. Sioux. c. 1890

Hair decorations: Sioux, Blackfoot, Sioux.
c. 1870-80

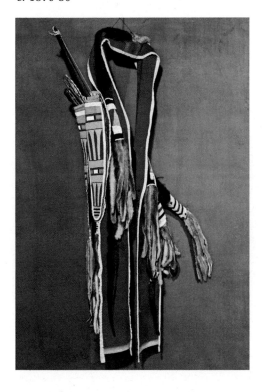

Bow case and quiver. Crow. c. 1870

Sioux shirt The painted and beaded deer-hide shirt on page 106 belonged to Joseph White Coyote, Oglala Sioux, of Manderson, South Dakota. It is decorated with quill-wrapped scalplocks. The necklace is made of bear claws and eagle talons, interspersed with assorted types of beads.

Hair decorations Hair decorations of different types (left) were worn as personal adornments and usually had a symbolic meaning. They may have represented war deeds, the unmarried status of a young man, membership in a military society, or tribal authority; or they may have served as personal medicines.

Crow bow case and quiver The Plains Indian bow case and quiver were attached to each other, an arrangement less cumbersome than carrying two separate items while on the hunt or in combat. They were worn without a shirt for greater freedom of movement.

The elaborate matched set from the Crow tribe (left, below) is made of otter skins and decorated with bands and pendants of ornamental beadwork; the shoulder sling is made of trade cloth.

Sioux bow case and quiver Plains Indian bows were rather short—approximately three feet in length—for easy handling on horseback; they are often referred to as "horse bows." Illustrated on page 85 is a Sioux bow case and quiver. A relatively early example, it is decorated with quill- and beadwork, and trimmed with fringe.

Crow dresses The matching pair of dresses illustrated on page 108 belonged to a Crow mother and her daughter. Made of trade cloth, they are typical of the reservation period. The decorations on the dresses are imitation elk teeth. Since only the two lower incisors of each wapiti elk were usable, the number of teeth was augmented by imitation teeth carved from the antlers.

Although the Crows were the probable originators of the idea, the Blackfeet also carved imitation elk teeth for dress decoration. In earlier times, genuine incisors were used when available and were highly valued as a trade item. Among the Crows, the trade value of a horse was equivalent to one hundred elk teeth.

◄ Dresses. Crow. c. 1890-1900

Woman's dress. Shoshoni or Kiowa (?). c. 1880-90 ▶

Shoshoni or Kiowa dress   Plains Indian women's dresses were generally made from three pieces of hide: one for the yoke, which hung like a cape over the shoulders and arms; and two large pieces for the body of the skirt, with the side seams fringed and sewn.

The dress on page 109, of soft tanned deer hide, lacks the capelike yoke but has a seam across its waist. Extending from each shoulder projection are two partially fringed pieces of hide that are sewn on the underside of the arm, forming sleeves. An additional fringed piece of hide in the shape of a long isosceles triangle is sewn between each of the side seams; two rows of tin-cone danglers are attached to the bottom of each hide panel.

The upper portion of the dress is decorated with both genuine and imitation elk teeth. The lower part of the skirt has thong pendants with assorted glass beads and is ornamented with cowrie shells. Cowries are small marine snails found in tropical waters and having highly polished, glossy shells. Only a limited number of species are found along the coastline of the United States: one Pacific species in southern California, and four Atlantic types in Florida. Cowrie shells were obtained by the Plains Indians through intertribal trading over long distances. Primitive people throughout the world (especially in Africa and Asia) have used cowrie shells for money, personal adornment, ornamentation of objects, and as religious symbols.

Cradles   Contrary to popular belief, there was no single, universal Indian word for either "cradle" or "baby." Words and names varied from tribe to tribe, according to individual dialects. In the northeastern United States, the Narragansett Indians (of the Algonquian linguistic stock) used the word *papùes* as the name for a little child. White settlers in the area interpreted the word as "papoose," and it came into widespread use with the migration westward. Consequently, white men today commonly refer to any Indian baby as a "papoose," and any type of cradle is called a "papoose carrier."

The Plains Indian baby usually spent the first year of its life in some type of cradle, which served as a means of protection, a sleeping place, and a method of transportation.

The practice of women carrying infants on their backs was common among primitive people throughout North America and in various other parts of the world. Among Plains Indian women, animal skins, buffalo robes, and portions of old tipi covers probably served as the earliest baby carriers. Exactly when cradles came into use on the Plains is uncertain, but historically they may be a relatively recent development. In the early days, a number of tribes, including the Assiniboin, Blackfeet, Plains Cree, and Southern Cheyenne, seem to have made little or no use of cradles.

Cradles of several distinctive styles existed on the Plains. Available materials and the surrounding environment account in part for the different cradle designs. Intertribal influences probably affected the dissemination of styles.

Flat, rectangular board cradles, showing the influence of the Woodland Indians to the east, were used by such tribes as the Pawnee, Iowa Osage, and some of the Eastern Sioux. The upper portions of these cradles were often decorated with carved and painted designs. Brass tacks were also occasionally used for ornamentation. A projecting footrest was attached to one end of the board, and fastened near the other end was a wooden-bow face guard. The face guard extended several inches in front of the infant's forehead, protecting it from injury if the cradle accidentally overturned. Two narrow decorative strips, made of quill- or beadwork, were sometimes added to the front of the cradle; these were several inches apart, extending vertically from the face guard to the footrest. After swaddling, the baby's body was completely bound to the cradle with colorful wraps of quill- or beadwork that were tightened in back by buckskin lacing thongs. A strap attached to the cradle was worn across the mother's forehead when she carried the infant on her back.

Hurdle cradles, used by the Yuman tribes of the Southwest, were also made by the Wichita and Southern Ute Indians. This type consisted of a bent willow frame in an oblong shape, with a backing of long narrow sticks lashed tightly together with thongs. The Wichita used bent-stick face guards, and bound the baby to the cradle with narrow, colorful woven sashes tied in back. The Southern Utes employed buckskin covers over the frame and used twine-woven wicker hoods.

A cradle unique among the Plains tribes was made by the Northern Arapaho of central Wyoming. The basic framework probably developed as a consequence of their contacts with the Southwest or Basin areas. Constructed from a bent willow branch, the frame was in the shape of a long, narrow inverted U with notched ends; a short transverse stick was placed in the notches across the opening of the U and tied into position with thongs. Strips of hide or trade cloth were tied across the bent willow frame to reinforce its shape. The frame was then placed on the inside of the cradle cover and fastened to it with a series of thongs. The cradle cover was usually made from a single piece of soft tanned deer hide, although sometimes a trade blanket or trade cloth, cut proportionally, was used. A protective hood was formed at the top of the cradle cover, and the lower portion was wrapped around the infant and tied with narrow quill-wrapped buckskin or rawhide thongs. The disk on the hood and the decorative rawhide bands around the edge of the cradle cover were adorned with quillwork, a characteristic feature of the Northern Arapaho cradle even after the introduction of glass beads. Some authorities claim that this was the only type of cradle made by the Arapaho, and that other styles attributed to them were actually gifts from other tribes.

Board cradles with the framework in the shape of an inverted U at the top and tapering toward the bottom were used by the Blackfeet, Crow, Shoshoni, Northern Ute, Kutenai, and Nez Percé. With the exception of those in the Crow style, these cradles were basically ovoid, and the baby was laced into a hooded skin pocket with a vertical opening; Nez Percé cradles sometimes had a decorative, triangular flap tied over the lacing. Northern Ute cradles used a twine-woven wicker hood instead of a skin hood. Crow cradles were more distinctive. They were oblong in shape and had three pairs of horizontal body bands to hold the infant securely.

Lattice cradles, the framework of which consisted of two narrow flat boards taper-

111

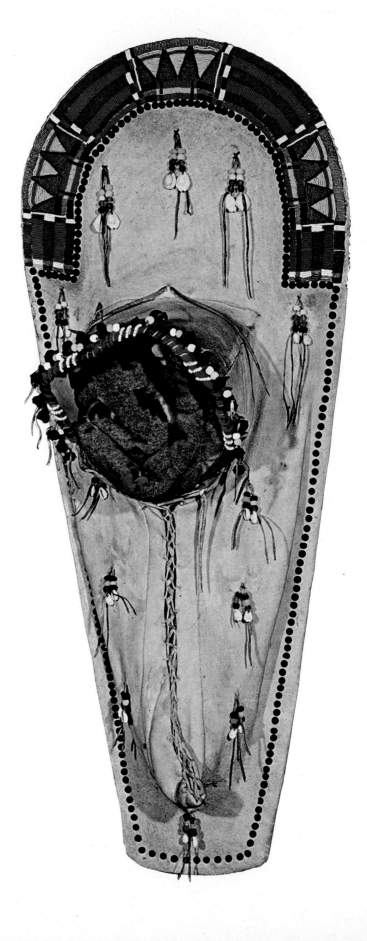

left: Board cradle with inverted "U" framework. Northern Ute. c. 1870-80. *right:* Board cradle with inverted "U" framework. Nez Percé. c. 1870

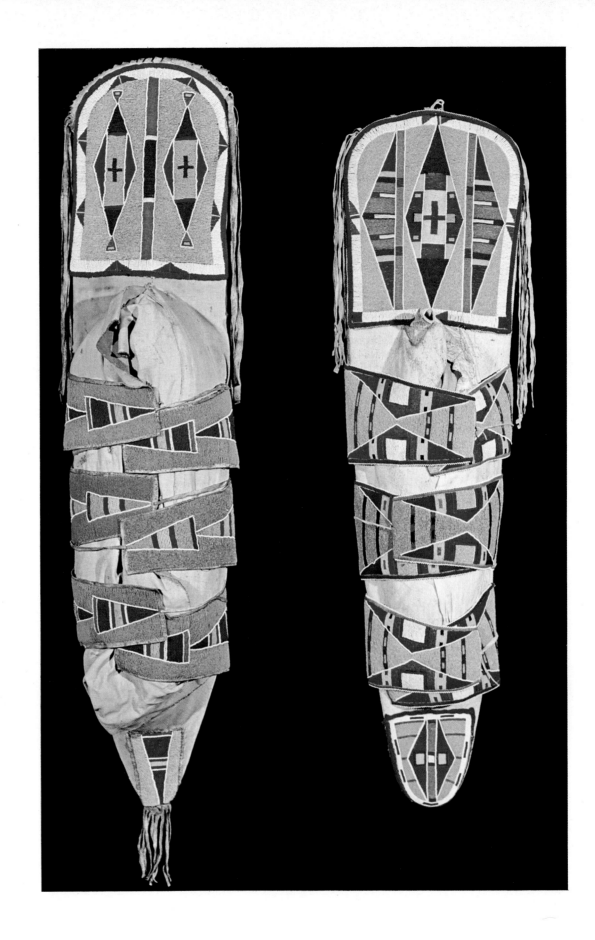

Board cradles with distinctive oblong shape and horizontal body
bands. Crow. c. 1870–80

ing toward the bottom in the shape of a modified V, were used by the Sioux, Cheyenne, Arapaho, Kiowa, and Comanche. The frame was held in position by narrow transverse boards lashed to it with buckskin thongs. The pointed ends of the flat sticks, often decorated with brass tacks, projected above the cradle case. The case, made from a single piece of deerskin and reinforced with a backing of rawhide, was lashed to the lattice frame. Rawhide was also used to reinforce the hood of the case, and the inside was sometimes completely lined with trade cloth. Some of the cases were heavily decorated on the outside with quill- or beadwork. Others were only partially decorated in this fashion; in these a piece of hide or trade cloth was sewn on to form the lower portion of the case. The vertical opening was held shut with a series of strings which were tied rather than laced.

Hood cradles were another type used by the Sioux, Cheyenne, and Arapaho. These cradles, which were not mounted on lattice boards, were made with a triangular hood, or a skin cover with hood and sides decorated with quill- or beadwork. A projecting oblong tab was sewn to the back of the hood, and the unattached corners were fastened with thongs to hold the hood in position. Sewn to the triangular hood or skin cover was a piece of hide or trade cloth, open on the botton, used as a body wrapping for the infant; tie strings held the cover shut. The cradle was held in the mother's arms, not carried on her back.

A cradle was made as comfortable as possible for the infant by means of padded bedding and a pillow. While natural contact with the pillow distorted the head of the baby to a degree, intentional artificial head deformation was not generally practiced by the Plains Indians. The Salish Indians of northwestern Montana, although they were commonly known as Flatheads, did not flatten their heads. Other tribes of the Salishan linguistic family along the Columbia River to the west used a cone-shaped wicker headboard attached to the cradles to compress the heads of their infants into a peak. They therefore considered the Salish, whose heads were normal in shape, to be flatheaded.

The bedding inside the cradles consisted of soft animal skins, downy feathers from birds, small blankets, or trade cloths. Juniper, shredded cottonwood bast, cattail down, soft moss, and scented herbs were used as absorbent, disposable diapers. The Arapaho packed thoroughly dried and finely powdered buffalo or horse manure between the baby's legs to serve as a diaper and prevent chafing. Cradles were cleaned and aired as frequently as the infant's diapers were changed.

Before the birth of the baby, it was the responsibility of the expectant mother, or one of the grandmothers, to make a small ornamented amulet in which the infant's umbilical cord would be preserved. The pouches, made of soft hide and decorated with quill- or beadwork, were usually in the shape of turtles and lizards (Sioux), snakes and horned toads (Blackfeet), or frogs and diamonds (Arapaho). Since the pouch was made during pregnancy, its shape and color did not indicate the sex of the child. The pouch was often hung on the cradle or around the infant's neck to protect him against evil spirits and to ensure long life. It remained a cherished possession from birth to death.

In addition to umbilical-cord pouches, small trinkets were often hung on the

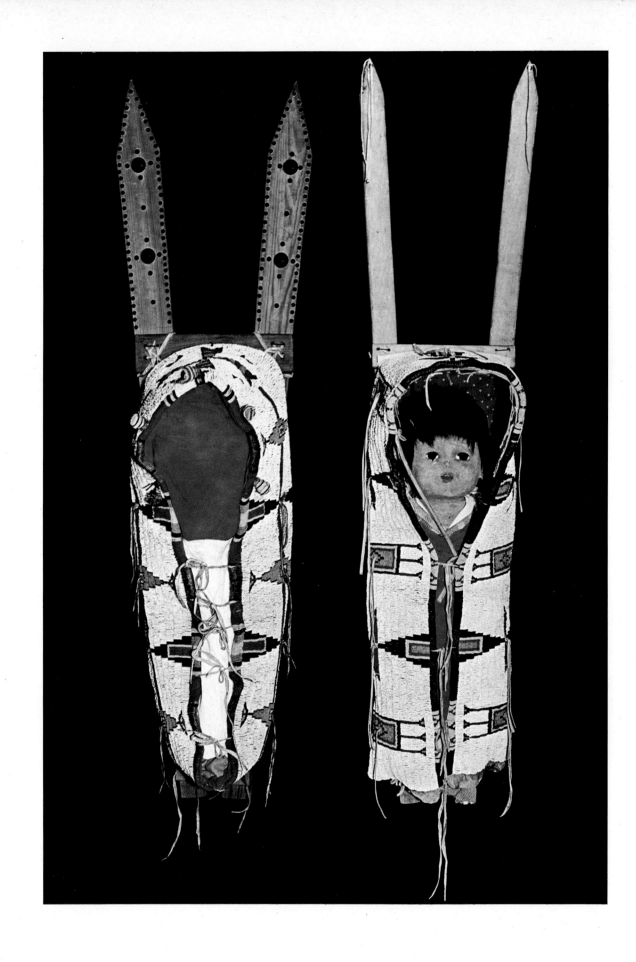

Lattice cradles with modified "V"
framework. Sioux. c. 1870–80

cradle for the baby's amusement. Cowrie shells, elk teeth, carved dewclaws, beaded pendants, brass cartridge casings, thimbles, coins, and any other number of small items were used as toys. If the cradle had a face guard, the trinkets were suspended from it; otherwise they were placed within reach of the baby's hands. When the cradle was not being transported, the infant was allowed to move his arms freely. When the cradle was carried on horseback, however, the baby's arms were securely held inside the cover to prevent injury.

The making of a beautifully decorated cradle was one of the most highly esteemed crafts of Plains Indian women. A cradle was often made not by the prospective mother but by a close female relative on her father's side of the family. Sometimes a woman who excelled in cradle-making would make a cradle in exchange for a horse or trade goods. Families often received several cradles as gifts, made as true labors of love. Once a family obtained a cradle it could never be sold, for fear that death would come to the child. If an infant died, he was often buried in the cradle; otherwise, it was destroyed or the mother kept it.

In his *Letters and Notes on the Manners, Customs, and Condition of the North American Indians,* published in 1841, the artist and writer George Catlin made the following observations concerning the use of mourning cradles among the Sioux Indians:

> The *mourning cradle* opens to the view of the reader another very curious and interesting custom. If the infant dies during the time that is allotted to it to be carried in this cradle, it is buried, and the disconsolate mother fills the cradle with black quills and feathers, in the parts which the child's body has occupied, and in this way carries it around with her wherever she goes for a year or more, with as much care as if her infant were alive and in it; and she often lays or stands it leaning against the side of the wigwam, where she is all day engaged in her needlework, and chatting and talking to it as familiarly and affectionately as if it were her loved infant, instead of its shell, that she was talking to. So lasting and so strong is the affection of these women for the lost child, that it matters not how heavy or cruel their load, or how rugged the route they have to pass over, they will faithfully carry this and carefully from day to day, and even more strictly perform their duties to it, than if the child were alive and in it.

A Plains Indian mother carried the cradle on her back by means of a buckskin carrying strap worn across her forehead or across her chest and upper arms. During journeys on horseback, the cradle was hung from the high pommel of the mother's saddle or was carried in a wicker basket attached to the poles of a *travois.* When the mother was working in camp, the cradle could be propped against the base of a tipi or hung from the limb of a tree.

Male and female Sioux deer-hide dolls The exceptionally fine Sioux dolls at left are made of deer hide and have beaded facial features. Human hair ornamented with porcupine-quill-wrapped hair decorations is attached to their heads. The dolls

Male and female deer-hide dolls. Sioux. c. 1885

Deer-hide doll. Sioux. c. 1875-80

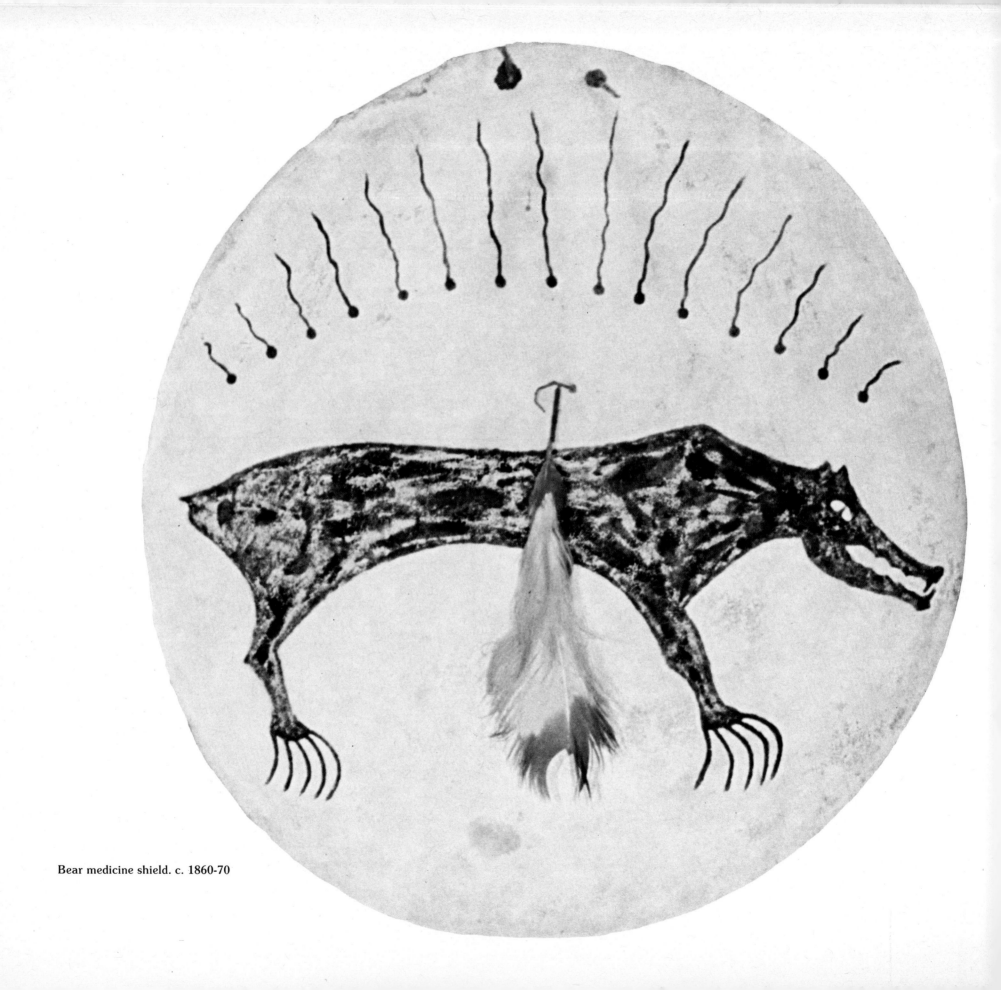

Bear medicine shield. c. 1860-70

Bear medicine case displaying articles used in rituals honoring the bear

are wearing moccasins with beaded soles. Some writers believe that doll moccasins were beaded on the bottom as an expression of sorrow at the death of the doll's owner.

Occasionally, a special pair of male and female dolls were used as love-medicine effigies. Their purpose was to attract a particular member of the opposite sex for the purpose of courtship and marriage, and they were included in unique, very personal medicine bundles.

Sioux deer-hide doll　Dolls were the principal toys used by little girls, especially those who were too young to help their mothers with chores around the camp. The doll on page 117, whose dress reproduces the details of adult costume with painstaking fidelity, was a true labor of love. The doll is made of deer hide, with human hair attached to the head. The face has beaded features and is painted with yellow ochre; spots of red ochre are on the cheeks. The earrings and the pendant on the small necklace are tiny snail shells. The dress, decorated with a fully beaded yoke, is worn with a beaded belt; a knife sheath and awl case are attached in back. A hairpipe necklace and beaded leggings and moccasins complete the outfit.

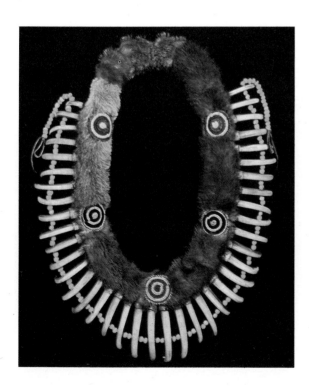

Bear-claw necklace. Sauk and Fox. c. 1840-50

Bear medicine case　The bear, particularly the grizzly, was highly respected by the Plains Indians. Regarded as one of the most sacred animals, the bear was revered for its strength, courage, wisdom, and healing powers. Many tribes believed they had descended from the bear. The bear often served as a *totem*, or sacred guardian spirit, for a clan or a single individual, and was frequently painted on shields, tipis, and other objects as a symbol of protection. Before battle, to protect themselves from harm, warriors frequently applied vertical stripes of red paint, signifying bear-claw marks, to their faces. The articles in the case (left, above) were used in honoring the bear, to gain the animal's supernatural powers.

The bear-knife medicine bundle, at the bottom of the case, is of Blackfoot origin. The bear knife was a highly valued, much-sought-after sacred medicine which made a warrior courageous and aggressive in battle. There were several individually owned bear-knife bundles among the Blackfeet. Obtaining a bear knife involved a dangerous transfer ceremony. Only two men, the owner and the initiate, took part in the ritual. After purification in the sweat lodge, sacred rites honoring the bear were performed in the owner's tipi. The transfer of the bear knife was the climax of the ceremony. Holding the sharp, double-edged knife by the blade, the owner threw the deadly weapon at the initiate. If the latter failed to catch the knife, he lost all claim to the war medicine. If the initiate caught the knife, however, he became the new owner and gained possession of its sacred powers.

The last owner of the bear knife in the Plains Indian Museum's collection was Three Calf, who is shown in the photograph holding the sacred knife.

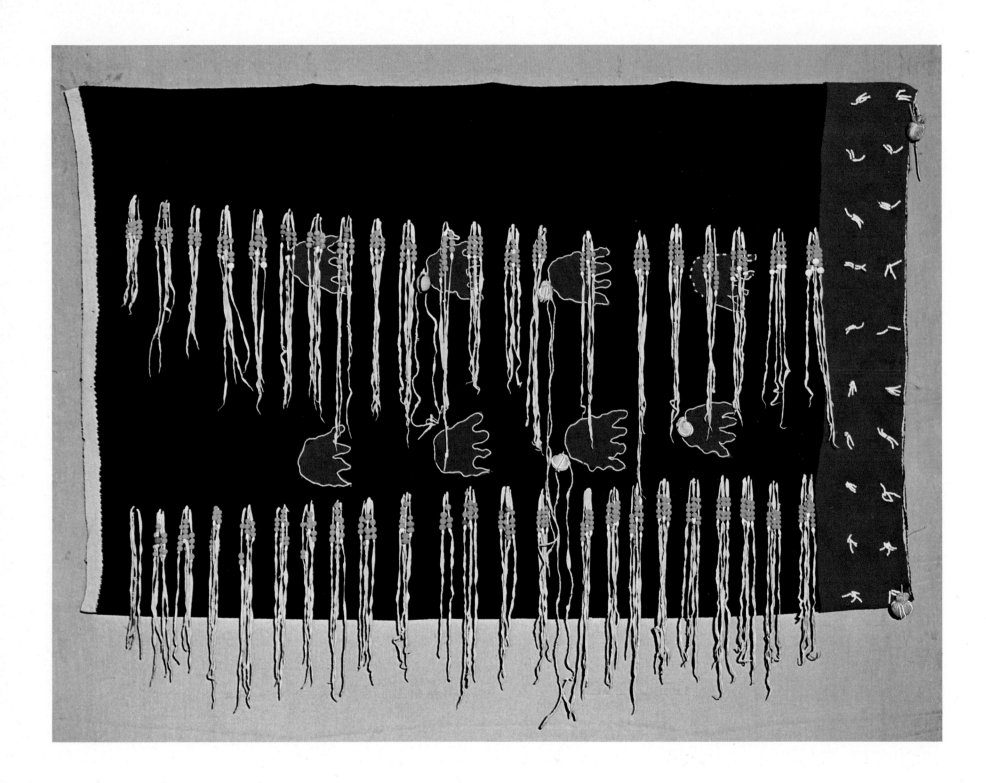

Bear-society flag, an insignia typical of the Omaha and the Pawnee. c. 1865

Bear medicine shields are arranged in an arc at the top of the case. (See also enlargement on page 118.) A circular shield of buffalo hide was one of the most sacred and valued possessions of the Plains Indian warrior. The design and decoration on the shield invested it with the protective powers of the "shield spirit." It was believed that these shields had the supernatural powers of the grizzly bear and would protect the owner from the weapons of his enemies.

Displayed on the bottom of the case behind the bear-knife medicine bundle is a Horse Dance stick. The ceremonial dance stick was carved by a warrior to honor a favorite war-horse killed in battle. The notched marks, painted in red, indicate where the animal was wounded.

Sauk-and-Fox bear-claw necklace   The bear-claw necklace on page 119 is one of the finest of its kind in existence. The long, beautifully matched claws are of the Great Plains grizzly, which has been extinct for a great many years. The necklace, which is more than a hundred years old, was worn by John Young Bear, medicine chief of a bear clan of the Sauk-and-Fox tribe.

Bear society flag   The trade-cloth appliqué flag on page 120 was the insignia of a bear society. The design, representing bear tracks, is typical of the Omaha and the Pawnee. The appliqué decoration was made by cutting pieces of red trade cloth into designs and sewing them onto the dark blue material. Attached to the flag are six small medicines and buckskin thong pendants with light blue globular beads.

Crow crupper for horse   Ornamented horse cruppers were both decorative and functional. On festive occasions both men's and women's horses were outfitted with cruppers as a display of beauty. On the march, cruppers (and breast collars) were used on horses and pack animals to hold the saddle in position and to prevent the loads from shifting. Early cruppers (and breast collars) were generally made of narrow bands of rawhide and were painted with geometric designs. Later styles were wider and usually included beaded decorations.

The crupper at left is made of commercially tanned leather foresections and deerskin rear sections. It is trimmed with beadwork, trade cloth, fringe, and pewter-spoon danglers. The front ends of the crupper were attached to the saddle with buckskin thongs. The narrow band connecting the two rear sections passed under the horse's tail. The crupper extended horizontally around the horse's hindquarters, with the fringe and pewter spoons hanging down.

Horse crupper. Crow. c. 1880-85

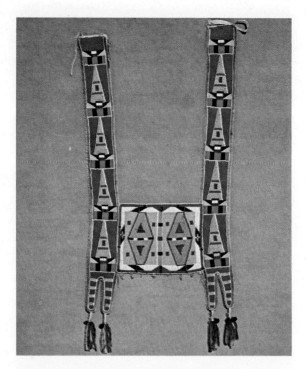

Horse's neck decoration. Crow. c. 1880

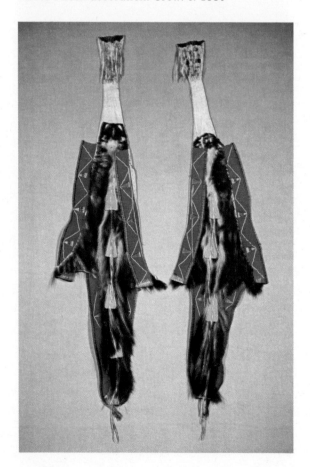

Skunk-hide horse's neck decoration. Crow. c. 1860-70

Crow horse's neck decoration   The elaborate Crow horse's neck decoration (left, above) has characteristic beadwork on a background of red trade cloth. Such decorations served no utilitarian purpose; they were used solely for ornamentation. Neck decorations of this style probably developed during the reservation period, when they were generally used only on women's horses. Since then, it has become fashionable to use neck decorations (and cruppers) on the riding horses of both sexes for parades and other celebrations.

Crow horse's neck decoration made from skunk hides   This unique horse's neck decoration (left, below) is made from two skunk hides. They are sewn onto red flannel trade cloth which is trimmed with narrow borders of green cloth and outlined with a single row of white seed beads. The red cloth background is decorated with beaded isosceles triangles and with a lightning design. The neck tabs are made of muslin, with beadwork and rawhide fringe at the top. The green cloth pendants on the skunk hides are outlined with a single row of white seed beads and are laced with buckskin thongs. Both sections of the decoration were tied around the horse's neck with buckskin thongs.

The skunk is actually a comparatively clean animal. Its flesh was sometimes eaten by the Plains Indians to supplement their diet. Boys accasionally kept young skunks as pets until the animals reached maturity and wandered off. Skunk hides were sometimes made into pouches or used as personal medicines, and the Plains Indians often told stories in which the animal was a featured character.

Crow woman's saddle   Contrary to popular belief, the Plains Indians almost always used saddles when riding on horseback. The woman's saddle, with its high pommel and cantle, was particularly distinctive.

The construction of a woman's saddle was quite simple, utilizing only four pieces of green cottonwood—two for the sideboards and two forked pieces for the pommel and cantle. After the pieces were cut, shaped, and smoothed, holes were burned into the forks and sideboards; these parts were aligned and laced into place with wet buckskin thongs. Then the whole frame was covered with wet buffalo rawhide, trimmed, and sewn with wet rawhide cord. Finally, the saddle was lashed onto a log to prevent warping as the rawhide dried and shrank.

The center-fire cinch rigging was equally simple: two rawhide straps which held rawhide cinch rings (metal rings were later obtained from traders) and a single rawhide cinch were laced to the outside of each of the sideboards

Stirrups were made of bent cottonwood and were covered with rawhide. A narrow strap of rawhide was looped through the bow of the stirrup and over the sideboards. The stirrup straps were adjusted for length and tied at the ends; they remained free to slide back and forth across the sideboards.

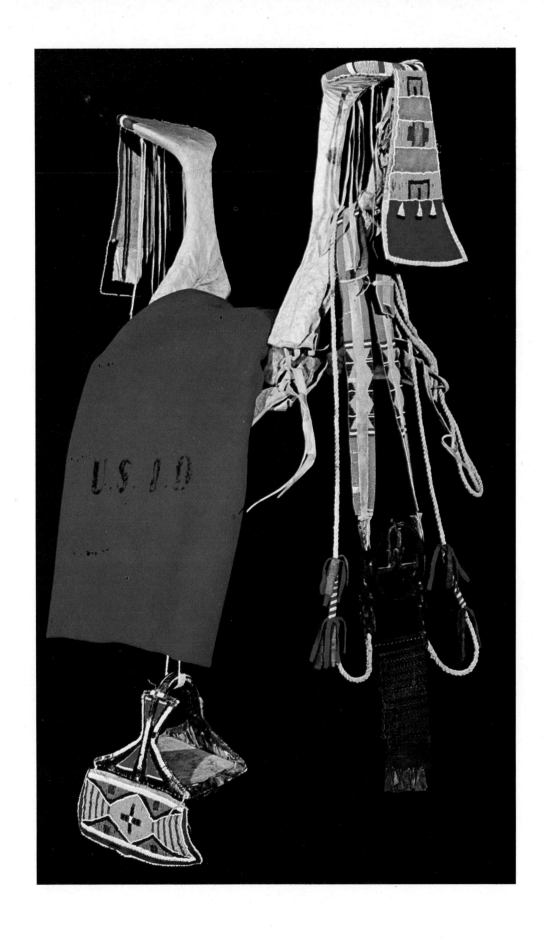

Woman's saddle. Crow. c. 1880–90

A distinctive feature of the woman's saddle was a hook that projected forward from the pommel. It was generally used to hold a cradle, quirt, or some type of container. Men used a pad saddle, which was made from two pieces of soft tanned animal skin stuffed with buffalo hair, or a low, forked saddle whose frame was made from elkhorn. The elkhorn saddle was known to the Blackfeet as "the prairie-chicken snare." Some early saddles utilized a suspended rawhide seat which was similar to ancient Hungarian rigs and to early U.S. Cavalry hussar saddles used during the War of 1812.

Plains Indians saddled and mounted their horses from the right, or "off," side. Saddle blankets were most frequently made from soft tanned buffalo hides; they were rectangular in shape, and the hair side was placed on the horse's back. Other types of soft hides, trade blankets, and canvas material were also used. The early types were undecorated, but late-nineteenth-century saddle blankets often had beaded borders (especially among the Sioux).

To provide added comfort for the rider, a buffalo robe or trade blanket was thrown over the saddle before mounting. Crow men were particularly fond of riding on fine mountain-lion hides. Women rode astride, a fact that was somewhat shocking to white observers, who were accustomed to seeing ladies of polite society riding sidesaddle.

Shown on page 123 is a wood-frame, rawhide-covered, Crow woman's saddle. The distinctive high pommel and cantle, which have flat, oval-shaped tops, are trimmed with beadwork and decorated with fringe. Beaded pendants hang from the pommel, cantle, and stirrups. The initials "U.S.I.D." on the government-issue blanket stand for "United States Indian Department." Hanging from the hook on the pommel is a beaded rawhide bridle with an old Spanish ring bit called a *chileno*.

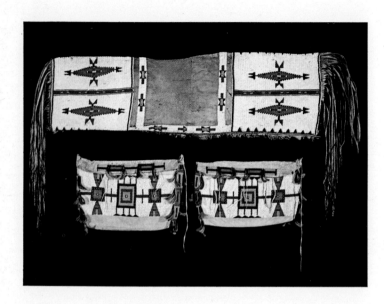

Saddlebags. Sioux. c. 1880–90

Sioux saddlebags   Saddlebags such as those illustrated at left were carried on the women's horses when moving camp. The long, rectangular, double saddlebag is made from two soft tanned elk hides sewn together in the middle. After the rectangular shape was cut, the hide was folded over and the outside edges were sewn together. A slit in the center of the saddlebag allowed items to be stuffed into either pocket. The saddlebag is decorated with beadwork, and the edges are trimmed with fringe. A buffalo robe or trade blanket was thrown over the saddlebag before mounting.

The beautifully matched pair of beaded saddlebags were used to carry a variety of items. They also served as an attractive decoration in the tipi.

Blackfoot sacred medicine bundles   Every facet of the culture of the Plains Indians was influenced by their religion. Prayers of offering and thanksgiving were a daily moral obligation. Some of the tribes were both monotheistic and animistic in their

Museum exhibit showing Sioux examples of porcupine quillwork, c. 1870-90, and Crow dresses and saddle, c. 1870-90

Museum exhibit showing Blackfoot medicine man and sacred medicine bundles of the Blackfoot people

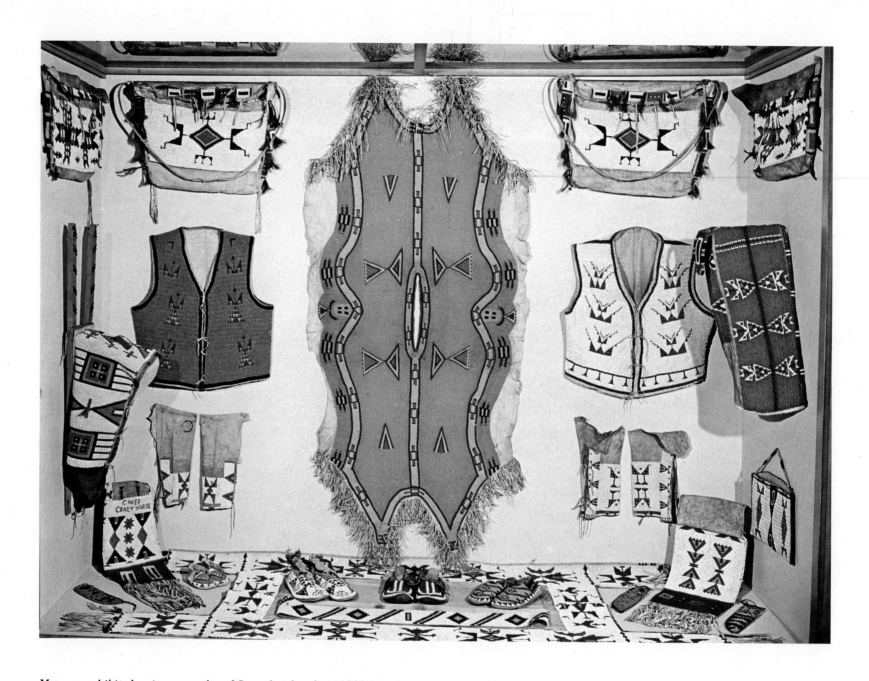

Museum exhibit showing examples of Sioux beadwork. c. 1880-90

religious beliefs. All aspects of life, nature, and the universe were viewed with wonder and respect. It was believed that all things created in the sky, on land, or below the water were created for a purpose, and possessed a supernatural power. Since they were capable of doing good or evil, the supernatural powers were both respected and feared. Offending them was thought to cause misfortune.

To face the uncertainty of everyday life with honor and dignity, and to ensure the success of all important undertakings, individuals sought supernatural power from a "sacred helper" during a "vision quest." Since the acquisition of supernatural power was especially important to all males, visions were sought by boys during adolescence and sometimes at as early an age as ten or twelve.

A vision seeker prepared for his quest by purifying himself in the sweat lodge. Then he left camp and traveled to an isolated location. Traveling alone and on foot, wearing only a breechclout and moccasins, he took neither food nor water and carried no weapons. His destination was high in the mountains, where he could be closer to the Creator. Arriving at the chosen site, he constructed a bed of flat rocks. He then placed himself in a reclining position facing east, one of the four cardinal directions, to greet the morning sun. Unless a vision was received earlier, he would remain at the site for the next four days and nights, praying and fasting, without sleep. The seeker continued this regimen of self-sacrifice until he had a vision—or collapsed from exhaustion. It was hoped that the supernatural powers would be compassionate and send him a vision or a dream. If the young seeker was deemed worthy of compassion, a sacred helper, usually a living member of nature's kingdom or a celestial force, would appear to him (sometimes in anthropomorphic form) and show him sacred objects which symbolized the supernatural power. The sacred helper would tell the seeker how to make and care for these objects and how he should use them to bring him success and protection throughout his earthly life. The seeker was taught sacred prayers, songs, and war cries and was told what colors or designs should be painted on his face, shield, and horse when riding into battle. He was instructed in the sacred obligations, taboos, and rituals required to obtain the good will of the spirit and warned of the consequences if he failed to perform these duties. He was told that all these "personal medicines" would serve him throughout life, if he would serve them until his death. From this time on, the sacred helper would share its supernatural power with the youth and act as his guardian spirit.

After the vision was received, the fast was broken and the youth returned to camp to make his sacred medicine bundle. Sometimes medicine men or some wise elders of the tribe would be consulted to obtain a correct interpretation of the vision and the proper procedure for making the bundle.

The medicine bundle contained the objects that had been revealed by the sacred helper in the vision (see museum exhibit on page 125). These objects were not the spirit itself, but were symbolic of the spirit, and they could only be employed successfully with the proper knowledge and reverence. To keep the guardian spirit near, one of the personal medicines was often worn as a neck or hair decoration, especially when preparing for battle.

Sioux beadwork A form of personal adornment which dates back to the Stone Age, beads have been made of all sorts of animal, mineral, and vegetable substances. Various types of beads have been discovered in many important archaeological excavations throughout the United States, including several sites in the Great Lakes region (copper: 3000 B.C.); burial mounds of the Red Ocher people in Illinois (shell and copper. 1000 B.C.); the Norton Mounds near Grand Rapids, Michigan (copper beads and shell ornaments: 400 B.C.); the Hopewell burial mounds in Ohio (silver from Canada and native copper from Wisconsin: 100 B.C.); and Pueblo Bonito in the Chaco Canyon, New Mexico (shell and turquoise: A.D. 1000–1200). The Indians of the Texas Panhandle Pueblo culture traded flint for shell beads about A.D. 900.

The decorative glass beads displayed on the items in the photo on page 126, however, were not made by the Plains Indians but were obtained through trade with white men.

Until about 1850, the glass factories of the town of Murano in the lagoon of Venice supplied white men with the majority of glass beads they traded to the Indians on the North American continent. After that date, glass beads began to be imported to America from Bohemia (now part of Czechoslovakia) and France. (There were several attempts at establishing a bead-making industry in the American Colonies, but these enterprises proved to be short-lived; by 1800 the making of glass beads had been abandoned for the more lucrative manufacture of window glass and bottles.)

The beads the white men traded to the Indians were made in long, thin tubes, which were cut into small sections. These sections were then polished and rounded in a mixture of sand and wood ashes. After they were removed from the mixture, the holes of the beads were cleaned out. The beads were then packaged and sent into the field by the various fur companies in casks, boxes, or barrels. Some were strung, and others were traded by the bulk or by the pound. (The practice of bead-making goes back to antiquity. The earliest known glass beads were made in Mesopotamia about 2600 B.C. These beads, which were carved rather than molded, are also the oldest known form of man-made glass. Beads were also made in ancient Egypt, and about 1540 B.C. the Egyptians developed molded glass, using a core of sand. Both the Mesopotamians and the Egyptians wore decorative glass-beadwork amulets.)

The Crow were among the first of the Indians of the Northern Plains to utilize beadwork for decoration, using blue glass beads as early as 1805. They obtained their beads from the Shoshoni, who had gotten them from the Spaniards of the Southwest.

The use of glass beads on the Plains was quite limited until 1835–40, and did not become widespread until after 1850. "Pony beads," which received their name from the pack animals that carried trade goods into the field, were introduced on the Plains in the early 1800s. These beads were about an eighth of an inch in diameter and were opaque; they were usually white, but also came in other colors, including black, blue, and red.

Seed beads, which were in use on the Plains in 1840–50, were about a sixteenth of an inch in diameter. They were used in decorating all types of Plains Indian paraphernalia and came in a variety of colors. Seed beads were opaque until about 1870, when translucent ones were introduced.

Flower blanket. Mesquakie. c. 1860-80

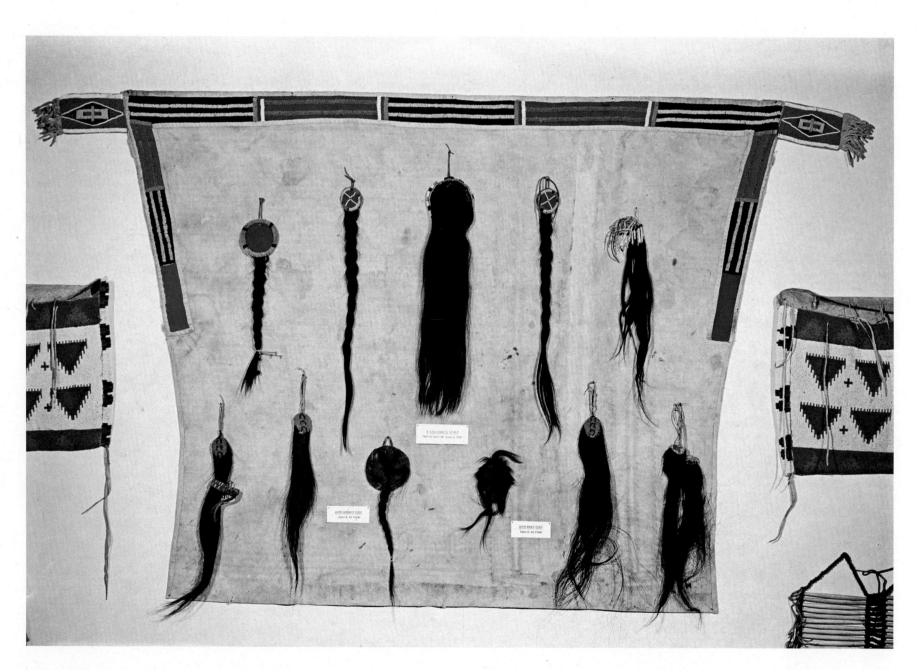

Human scalps displayed on Crow saddle blanket

The earliest beadwork of the Plains Indians was quite simple in design, utilizing narrow borders, blocks, bands, and rectangles. As time progressed, designs became more intricate, and by the reservation period complex geometric patterns were common.

Although needles and thread became a trade item soon after beads were introduced, buffalo and deer sinew were often preferred to thread because of their strength and durability.

The most common beadwork techniques employed were the lazy stitch and the overlay stitch. In the lazy stitch an awl or needle was used to pierce the hide, and the beads were strung in short parallel rows; because the sinew or thread did not go entirely through the hide, no stitching was visible on the back side. The beads did not lie flat, but had a small rise in them. This technique did not lend itself to curvilinear forms.

In the overlay stitch, two needles and thread were employed: one to string the beads and the other to make the stitches. Fewer beads were strung at one time, and the stitches were made closer together, producing a smooth effect. Curvilinear forms were easily achieved with this technique.

Beadwork designs generally had an artistic rather than symbolic purpose, although certain designs may have had a special symbolism for the owner. Also, the same design might mean something entirely different to a man than it would to a woman. Because beadwork designs were at times copied from tribe to tribe, it often becomes difficult to distinguish between Crow and Nez Percé, or Sioux and Northern Cheyenne. Colors more often had symbolic meanings, but these meanings varied in different tribes.

Many other varieties of trade beads—polychrome, paternoster, brass, faceted— were used for making necklaces. Bone hairpipes, a trade item manufactured in New Jersey, were strung vertically for a woman's necklace and horizontally for a man's breastplate.

Human scalps displayed on Crow saddle blanket Taking scalps as trophies of war was practiced in Asia by the ancient nomadic Scythians as long ago as the fifth century B.C. In Europe, scalping was a custom of the ancient Franks and Visigoths. Scalping was also practiced in some limited areas of the New World in Pre-Columbian days, but even in historic times it was not common among the majority of North American Indians.

Scalping was introduced in the eastern United States during the early Colonial period, when the government offered bounties for the scalps of men, women, and children of certain unfriendly Indian tribes. During the French and Indian War (1754–63) the French offered bounties for British scalps. The British then retaliated by offering bounties for the scalps of both the French and their Indian allies. Bounties were being occasionally collected by scalp-hunters on the Western frontier as late as the middle of the nineteenth century.

The origin and significance of scalping among the Plains Indian tribes is question-

Sioux quilled vest left on the Wounded Knee battlefield, South Dakota, on December 29, 1890

able. While scalping may have been practiced by some tribes, such as the Blackfeet, before the introduction of horses and firearms, the custom was probably unknown to many of the tribes until comparatively recent times, when it undoubtedly developed in response to the barbarity of white scalp-hunters.

Scalps were often taken by war parties as a reprisal against enemies that had killed prominent leaders or warriors in battle. Scalping was painful, but not necessarily fatal. Usually only a small circular portion of hair and skin, several inches in diameter, was taken; this included the "scalplock" in back of the crown. The scalplock symbolized a man's life, and as a trophy of war proved the prowess of the victor. Occasionally, if time permitted, the entire head was scalped; the locks of hair removed were frequently used for decorating war shirts, leggings, and other items. Often the victim was scalped by someone other than the person who had wounded or killed him.

Sometimes, as a sign of tribal defiance, a captured enemy was scalped alive and released to return to his tribe in disgrace. Men who survived the shame of being scalped usually covered their bald spots with some type of headgear. Scalps were not always preserved; sometimes they were left at the scene of battle as an offering to a sacred deity.

Only a war party that had not lost any men in battle returned home in a display of triumph. Bearing enemy scalps, the warriors rode into camp with their faces painted black as a symbol of victory. The warriors presented the scalps to their female relatives, who carried them, stretched on wooden hoops attached to long poles, in a victory ceremony known as the Scalp Dance. The ceremony, which was held in the center of the camp circle, lasted anywhere from one to fifteen nights. All participants wore black face paint during the numerous songs and dances of this triumphant celebration. After the Scalp Dance, the scalps, having served as a symbol of revenge and prowess, were sometimes buried.

While taking scalps became common among the Plains Indians, most tribes placed greater importance on "counting coup" in battle. The term *coup* (koo), derived from the French-Canadian trapper's word meaning "a blow" or "sign of victory," originally signified that a warrior had touched an enemy's body in combat. Later, "coup" was applied to other deeds of valor. A public recital of war exploits was known as "counting coup." During these recitals, a warrior spoke only of his victories, never of his defeats. Absolute truthfulness was required at all times. False information would be challenged, and a warrior that lied would lose status; death would surely follow him or a member of his family.

Constant intertribal warfare was a way of life for the Plains Indians. Defensive and economic reasons aside, intertribal hostilities enabled a man to earn honors for courage displayed in battle. For each coup counted, a man scored a point in the war-honor system. The more points a man accumulated, the more status he had as a warrior.

The ranking of war honors varied from tribe to tribe. A coup of primary importance in one tribe may have been regarded as a deed of secondary rank in another.

Touching an enemy was regarded as one of the bravest war deeds, and was considered more bold than killing or scalping. If the enemy had not been felled, it meant having to expose oneself to danger while sparing the enemy's life. Being the first to

Museum exhibit showing pipes and pipe bags. c. 1870-90

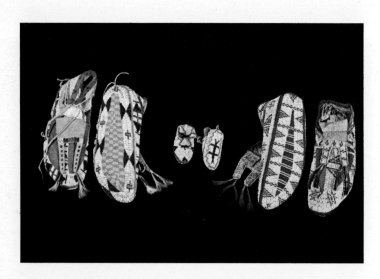

Moccasins with beaded soles. Cheyenne. c. 1880-90

touch a fallen enemy also required courage since the results could be fatal if he was only feigning death. Some warriors rode into battle armed only with a coup stick to make the touch. The coup stick was a special curved staff approximately six feet long, usually wrapped with otter fur and decorated with eagle feathers signifying war honors. The touch could also be made with the bare hand, a bow, lance, quirt, or gun. The Cheyenne allowed three different warriors to touch the same enemy; the Arapaho, Sioux, Assiniboin, and Crow permitted four men to strike blows. The warrior who made the first touch received the highest honor, with the others ranked in descending order.

Killing was also a deed of valor, with a kill made in hand-to-hand combat ranking higher than one made with a bow or gun from a safe distance. Scalps were highly prized by the Sioux and the Cree, but among many other tribes the degree of respect for an enemy's prowess determined the value of his scalp as a trophy of warfare. Capture of an enemy's weapons such as a bow, lance, war club, tomahawk, knife, or gun, was an important coup. Captured warbonnets, shirts, moccasins, and other articles of clothing were also prized; these were sometimes worn as disguises during horse raids into enemy camps. Stealing horses and mules was another exploit deserving of merit. This common practice was considered especially bold if the animal was tethered near an enemy tipi; striking the tipi also ranked as a coup. Rescuing an endangered companion from death was an act of valor, but to desert a friend was a disgrace. Leading a successful war party without loss of men in battle was a highly esteemed honor.

Blackfoot Sacred Thunder medicine pipe   The sacred medicine pipe illustrated on page 86 was a gift to the Blackfoot people from the Thunder. It possessed healing powers and provided protection for the people.

Shortly after the first sound of thunder was heard every spring, the sacred medicine-pipe bundle was opened in a solemn ceremony to renew its healing powers. Of all the important items included in the medicine bundle, the elaborately ornamented pipestem, with ermine skins, quill- and beadwork, feathers, and bells, is the most sacred.

Cheyenne moccasins with beaded soles   Some Plains stories teach that moccasins with beaded soles were burial moccasins, made to enable the deceased to walk on the clouds and travel beyond the skies to join his relatives in the Always Summer Land. But such moccasins, which displayed the craftsmanship and generosity of the maker, were not made exclusively for the dead. Old photographs (for example, F. A. Rinehart's full-length portrait of the Sioux chief American Horse, taken in 1898) show living persons wearing them, and we are told that they were sometimes worn for weddings and other ceremonial occasions. On some present-day reservations young women make moccasins with beaded soles as keepsake gifts for their sweethearts.

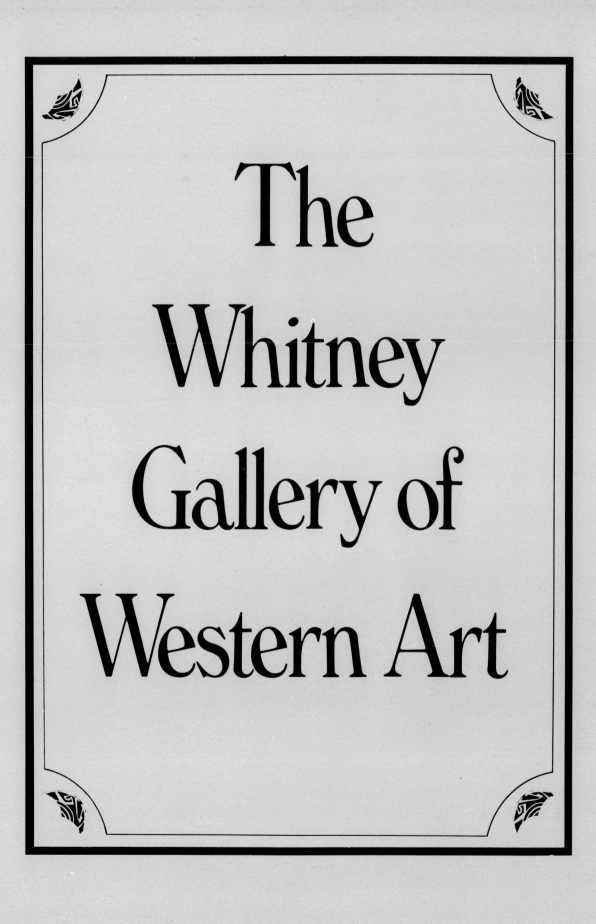

The Whitney Gallery of Western Art

Charles M. Russell.
Detail of *When Law Dulls the Edge of Chance.* 1915. Oil, 30 x 48″.
The William E. Weiss, Jr., Collection in the Whitney Gallery of
Western Art *(foldout)*

THE paintings and sculpture in the Whitney Gallery of Western Art have been selected for their documentary fidelity to the story of the Old West. Among the artists who recorded the West in paintings and sculpture were individuals of integrity and abundant talent. The significance of the large collection of the Whitney Gallery lies in its importance, both historic and artistic, as a repository of authentic Americana.

The Hudson River valley and pastoral New England provided inspiration for the early American painters in the East. But the West contained an even broader, more exciting and varied field for the artist. In the first quarter of the nineteenth century it was still largely inaccessible and dangerous. To the artist willing to endure hardship and danger, the attractions of the Hudson valley were infinitely multiplied in the vast wilderness of the West.

The great space, size, and energy which characterized the early West provided the first purely "American" experience of magnitude, and they laid the foundation for a clearly definable school of artistic expression: Western art—one which, significantly, has persevered through a century and a half.

What follows is not an attempt at a definitive work on the field of Western art. Rather it is specifically tailored to provide pertinent background information on the individual collections of the Whitney Gallery of Western Art. These collections range from the early period of Catlin, Miller, and Bierstadt, through the golden age of Remington and Russell, to the more recent efforts of such painters as Carl Rungius, Frank Tenney Johnson, and others. The Whitney Gallery thus affords a wide enough variety of Western art to serve as the basis for sound conclusions about the field as a whole. The fact that such a remarkable collection exists is a direct result of the foresight and dedication of the director emeritus of the Whitney Gallery of Western Art, Dr. Harold Mc-Cracken.

Artists
in the
Wilderness

Albert Bierstadt. Detail of *The Last of the Buffalo.*
1888. Oil, 60 x 96'' *(foldout)*

THERE WAS both promise and challenge as America confronted her vast inland empire early in the nineteenth century. The men who would venture into the unknown territory west of the Mississippi, and into the far reaches of the upper Missouri River, had to be cut from a fearless fabric.

Resourcefulness and independence were essential, for life in the prairies and mountains presented countless dangers. But there were men to meet the challenge. Among these were Lewis and Clark, who followed in the wake of the fiercely independent fur trappers, and were in turn followed by other explorers, trappers, and traders. In this company of rugged men were a few artists.

Among them were highly skilled, competent painters with backgrounds in the academies and salons of Europe. Most of these artists, however, were more concerned with the accurate representation of the new country than with creative expression. They were privileged, as few artists have been, to sketch and paint in a trackless virgin region; to be the first to capture both human and geographic subjects which no other artist had ever seen.

Their motives and their intentions varied. Alfred Jacob Miller accompanied Capt. William Drummond Stewart into the wilderness in 1837 as an exciting diversion from an unsuccessful career in New Orleans. Others, like George Catlin and John Mix Stanley, felt a compelling mission to record for posterity a land and a people uncorrupted by the onslaught of civilization. Samuel Seymour, the first to paint the Colorado Rock-

145

ies, and James Otto Lewis did their work for official reasons, as employees of the government.

But whatever their motives, these artists produced works that were to constitute a new "school" of art. It was genuine American art, and a major step toward cultural independence from the domination of European tradition. Some of the earliest painters in the West were Neoclassical in their style. This severe manner of painting, which developed in the wake of the French Revolution, was a reaction to the elaborate Rococo style, which reflected aristocratic tastes. The objectivity of Neoclassicism was well-suited to the early Western painters' aims. It lent itself admirably to chronicling the physical wonders of the still-mysterious American frontier. Their contribution would not have been so great or so enduring had they concentrated on their subjective impressions.

A few of the early painters of the West, such as Alfred Jacob Miller, Thomas Moran, and Albert Bierstadt, were more closely related to the French Romantics than to the Neoclassicists. Moran and Bierstadt were more concerned with grandiose mountain landscapes, which were a dominant part of the Western scene, than with the more mundane genre portrayals of life in the West. Both Neoclassicism and Romanticism played an important part in the development of a distinctive pattern for Western painting.

George Catlin. *Catlin Inside a Mandan Lodge.* Oil, 15⅜ x 21⅞". The Paul Mellon Collection, National Gallery of Art, in the Whitney Gallery of Western Art

George Catlin

George Catlin (1796–1872) began his professional life as an attorney. The Pennsylvania-born lawyer gave up his practice, however, and began a new career as a self-taught portrait miniaturist in 1821. By 1824 he was a member of the Pennsylvania Academy of the Fine Arts, which included the illustrious Peale family and Thomas Sully. In 1828 his work was exhibited by the American Academy of Fine Arts in New York.

As a result of seeing a delegation of Plains Indians on its way to Washington, Catlin conceived the idea of depicting on canvas all the tribes between the Alleghenies and the Rocky Mountains. He made his first Western excursion in 1832, traveling by steamboat by the Missouri, sketching and painting the Indians and landscapes all along the route from St. Louis to the mouth of the Yellowstone River.

In subsequent years he traveled to the Southwest (1834), the upper Mississippi River and Great Lakes region (1835–36), and the Carolinas (1837–38). Catlin visited forty-eight tribes and executed a remarkable number of genuine ethnological studies. Many of his nearly five hundred Indian portraits were published in 1841, to illustrate his *Letters and Notes on the Manners, Customs and Condition of the North American Indians.*

Few American artists have painted with Catlin's dedication to purpose. He found endless inspiration for his work of "rescuing from oblivion the looks and customs of the vanishing races of native men in America."

Catlin's greatest strength as an artist was his portraiture, though the paintings he executed in the field were more ethnologically than artistically oriented. The extremely difficult conditions under which he worked account for the rather primitive style of his field paintings. They are honest and direct in detail, however, and what they lack in aesthetic refinement is compensated for by their historical accuracy.

In his *Letters and Notes,* of 1841, Catlin expressed his mission and the essence of his inspiration:"Man, in the simplicity and loftiness of his nature unrestrained and unfettered by the disguises of art, is surely the most beautiful model for the painter—and the country from which he hails is unquestionably the best study or school of arts in the world: such I am sure, from the models I have seen, is the wilderness of North America. And the history and customs of such people, preserved by pictorial illustrations, are themes worthy of the life-time of one man, and nothing short of the loss of my life shall prevent me from visiting their country, and of becoming their historian." To this single purpose Catlin dedicated his artistic life.

Dr. Harold McCracken, in *George Catlin and the Old Frontier* (1952), assesses the artist's achievement: "It can be said with justice and justification that no other artist or writer in the field of the North American Indian and the Old West has had as long and broad an influence as George Catlin."

George Catlin. *One-Horn Head, Chief of the Sioux.* Oil, 15¼ x 21⅞". The Paul Mellon Collection, National Gallery of Art, in the Whitney Gallery of Western Art

George Catlin. *Buffalo Dance*. Oil, 17½ x 23½''. The Paul Mellon Collection, National Gallery of Art, in the Whitney Gallery of Western Art

George Catlin. *Cheyennes Starting on a Hunt.* Oil, 15¾ x 22¼". The Paul Mellon Collection,
National Gallery of Art, in the Whitney Gallery of Western Art

Karl Bodmer

Karl Bodmer (1809-1893) is most widely remembered for the works which were used to illustrate *Journey into the Interior of North America* (1839), by the German naturalist Maximilian, Prince of Wied. Bodmer, a native Swiss, was trained as an artist in Paris by his uncle, Johann Jakob Meyer von Meilen. At twenty-three he came to America with Maximilian, as official artist for a proposed expedition into the Far West.

The party left St. Louis in April of 1833, journeying up the Missouri on the steamboat *Yellowstone,* which George Catlin had traveled on a year earlier. From Fort Union the party went by keel boat to Fort McKenzie, the American Fur Company's outpost in the shadow of the eastern slope of the Rockies.

While at Fort McKenzie, Maximilian and the young artist found themselves in the midst of a fierce battle between the Blackfeet and the Cree. This provided the first opportunity for the Swiss painter to record Indian combat.

Most of the work Bodmer produced on the journey was done in watercolor. His subjects included Plains Indians, wild life, and landscapes. Eighty-two of these paintings were reproduced as aquatints to accompany Maximilian's two-volume narrative of the expedition.

Bodmer returned to France in 1834 and made his debut at the Salon in Paris in 1836. Thereafter he was a more or less regular exhibitor in Paris. He settled in the artists' colony at Barbizon, in the Fountainebleau Forest, where he exerted considerable influence. The young Jean François Millet executed several paintings from some of Bodmer's Western field sketches. The paintings were later reproduced as lithographs by Bodmer.

American art historians have written of Bodmer as if he produced nothing subsequent to his Indian paintings. He went on, however, to establish a fine reputation for his painting that was quite apart from his American experience. Little, if any, of the recognition he achieved in Europe resulted from his contributions to *Journey into the Interior of North America.* Writing in 1873, P. G. Hamerton said of Bodmer: "He is an artist of consummate accomplishment . . . and of immense range. . . . The bird or the beast is always the central subject with Karl Bodmer, but he generally surrounds them with a graceful landscape, full of intricate and mysterious suggestions . . . drawn with perfect fidelity and care."

The legacy of Western art was richer indeed because Karl Bodmer made the trip up the Missouri in 1833. He was one of the most accomplished and sophisticated artists to portray the early West.

Karl Bodmer. *Moennitarri (Hidatsa) Warrior in the Costume of the Dog Dance.* **Hand-colored lithograph, 25 x 18"**

Karl Bodmer. *Woman of the Snake Tribe—Woman of the Cree Tribe.* Hand-colored
lithograph, 18 x 25″

Karl Bodmer. *An Assiniboin Indian—A Yanktonan (Sioux) Indian.* Hand-colored
lithograph, 18 x 25''

Karl Bodmer. *A Mandan Chief.* Hand-colored lithograph, 21 x 14½

Alfred Jacob Miller

Alfred Jacob Miller (1810–1874) was among the first painters of the Old West. His work, primarily in watercolor, is characterized by dramatic situations and exotic subjects that remind one of the French Romantic painter Eugène Delacroix.

Miller was born in Baltimore and received his first art training in 1831–32 as a student of Thomas Sully. He had no particular interest in the American frontier as an artistic resource when he went to Europe to study in 1833. In Paris Miller attended the École des Beaux-Arts. Later he spent some time in Rome and Florence. He copied the old masters and seemed destined for a career of portraits and landscapes in the delicate style of the English painter J.M.W. Turner.

Upon his return to America in 1834, he set up a studio in Baltimore but for the next three years had only minimal success. In 1837 he moved to New Orleans and began to seek portrait commissions. After meeting Captain William Drummond Stewart, the Scottish sportsman and adventurer, in New Orleans, Miller joined him in an expedition to the West, thus forming an association like that between Maximilian and Bodmer.

They traveled overland with an American Fur Company caravan bound for the annual fur-trade rendezvous in the Green River valley of Oregon. From Fort Laramie, through the South Pass of the Rockies, and on to the valley of the Green River, Miller saw and portrayed the frontier of the mountain-man era in its fullest bloom. Kit Carson, Jim Bridger and a host of equally exciting trappers were on hand in that summer of 1837, along with nearly three thousand Indians of the golden age of Plains Indian culture.

Unlike George Catlin, Miller was a trained professional painter who was guided by the "art-for-art's-sake" credo. He romanticized the Western landscapes, mountain men, and Indians just as he would have a bayou scene in Louisiana.

Upon his return to New Orleans he began to execute paintings from his copious field sketches. Some of his finished paintings were exhibited in Baltimore and New York in 1838–39. Miller then went to Scotland for a year to execute commissions of the Western trek for Stewart. By 1842 he had resettled in Baltimore, where he was to spend the rest of his life doing portraits and re-creating countless scenes from his Western sketchbook. Miller's delicate technique and imaginative composition show him to be the first of the disciples of Romanticism to paint the Old West.

Alfred Jacob Miller. *Louis—Mountain Trapper.* Watercolor, 13 x 7″

Alfred Jacob Miller. *Trappers Saluting the Rocky Mountains.* Oil, 22 x 36″

Alfred Jacob Miller. *Indians Approaching Buffalo.*
Watercolor, 9 x 17″

Alfred Jacob Miller. *Snake Indians Pursuing Crows.* Watercolor, 8 x 15″

To Wind in his hair
Paw on his nose,
Since 12-23-99 we have
been inseperable. all time stands
still when I hold your hand . . .
forever I ♥ u my soul mate
Mother of all cats

8-13-13

Alfred Jacob Miller. *Indian Elopement.* Oil, 28 x 36″

Alfred Jacob Miller. *Our Camp*. Oil, 26½ x 36″

Alfred Jacob Miller. *The Lost Greenhorn.* Oil, 17⅝ x 24″

John Mix Stanley

John Mix Stanley (1814-1872) ranks with Catlin and Miller as a painter of the Western Indians. Born in Canandaigua, New York, he moved to Detroit as a young man and did sign painting to earn a living. He also set up a studio, however, and began his painting career in the late 1830s. Moving frequently, he attempted to establish his reputation as an artist. In 1842 he traveled overland into the Indian country and established a studio at Fort Gibson, in Arkansas Territory. After observing the Indian, Stanley found his calling in art. The International Indian Council, which was held at Tahlequah, Oklahoma Territory, in 1843, afforded Stanley an unparalleled opportunity to paint Indians. Prominent individuals from many tribes sat for him. His subsequent career was devoted entirely to Indian subjects.

Late in 1845 Stanley returned to the East and began to exhibit work from his Western sojourn. The paintings were well received, and by that summer he was back among the Indians. He accompanied a trading party to Santa Fe, and then joined a military expedition to California. He then moved on to Oregon, sketching and painting at every opportunity. After a side trip to Hawaii, where he painted King Kamehameha III and his queen, Stanley returned to the East.

He set up a studio in Washington, D.C., and in 1852 placed some two hundred of his paintings on exhibit at the Smithsonian Institution, hoping to interest the government in purchasing them to form the nucleus of a national Indian gallery. In 1853-54 he made his last trip into the West, as an artist for the Pacific Railroad survey. Although his paintings remained on loan to the Smithsonian, Congress failed to act on the purchase of the collection. Disheartened at this lack of interest, Stanley returned to Detroit in 1864. Further misfortune came in January 1865 when a disastrous fire in the Smithsonian destroyed all but five of his portraits.

Though he was perhaps the most widely traveled of all the early Western artists, John Mix Stanley died in 1872 in the same town where he had begun as a sign painter nearly forty years before. Many of his fine landscapes and genre works of the Indian country have survived, but he is primarily remembered as a portrait artist. His romantic attachment for the Indian is reflected in the idealized style of his painting. Stanley's obvious affection for his subjects helps make him second only to Catlin as a portrayer of the Indian in his natural state.

John Mix Stanley. *Last of Their Race.* Oil, 42 x 60″

Albert Bierstadt

Albert Bierstadt. *The Last of the Buffalo.* 1888. Oil, 60 x 96″

Albert Bierstadt (1830–1902) came to America from his native Germany at the age of two, and grew up in New Bedford, Massachusetts. He returned to Germany in 1853, to study at the Düsseldorf Academy. His teachers were Karl Friedrich Lessing, Andreas Achenbach, Emanuel Leutze, and the American landscape painter Worthington Whittredge. After traveling and painting in Switzerland and Italy, he returned to America in 1857.

In the summer of 1859 Bierstadt accompanied Col. Frederick William Lander's surveying expedition to the region of the western Rockies. His travels in the Swiss and Italian Alps sharpened his observations of the Rockies: In a letter to the art magazine *Crayon,* he wrote: "The mountains are very fine; as seen from the plains they resemble very much the Bernese Alps . . . . They are of a granite formation, the same as the Swiss mountains and their jagged summits, covered with snow and mingling with the clouds, present a scene which every lover of landscape would gaze upon with unqualified delight. As you approach them, the lower hills present themselves more or less clothed with a great variety of trees, among which may be found the cotton-wood, lining the river banks, the aspen, and several species of the fir and pine . . . . And such a charming grouping of rocks . . . . The manners and customs of the Indians are still as they were hundreds of years ago, and now is the time to paint them . . . . The color of the mountains . . . reminds one of the color of Italy . . ."

This first Western excursion determined the course of Bierstadt's subsequent career. He would do for the Western mountains what William Doughty, Thomas Birch, and Thomas Cole had done for those of the Hudson River valley. If a case is to be made for the existence of a Western school, in the sense of a Hudson River school, its earliest example would be the Rocky Mountain painters, with Albert Bierstadt as the father of the group.

Bierstadt's paintings were heroic in scope and strongly influenced by his Düsseldorf training. Their size and patriotic character brought him many lucrative government commissions, a fact which prompted Samuel Isham, a disgruntled contemporary, to observe: "When...Congress voted money for a work of art it was...a portrait of Washington or a landscape by Bierstadt."

His first major Rocky Mountain canvas was exhibited at the National Academy of Design in 1860, the same year in which he was elected to the academy. In the early 1860s, Bierstadt's paintings were selling for as much as $35,000, breaking all records in American art prices. By 1866 he was *the* American artist of the day, although the critics consistently deprecated his Romanticism.

Bierstadt built a huge studio-home on the Hudson above New York, and he and his wife entertained both upper-class Americans and European nobility in a lavish manner. In 1867 he took several of his mountain paintings on a grand tour of Europe. He was received and acclaimed by royalty in each country he visited.

Bierstadt continued his visits to the mountains of the West through the years. But American tastes in painting slowly began to change. Patrons started listening to the critics who touted the new French Impressionists. Romanticism was on its way out.

Albert Bierstadt. *A Wild Stallion.* Oil sketch, 13¼ x 19¼"

What was perhaps Bierstadt's finest painting, *The Last of the Buffalo* (see pp. 141–42, 162), was rejected by a committee of American artists appointed to select American paintings for the 1889 Paris Exposition. The dean of the Rocky Mountain painters died in New York in 1902, discouraged and alienated. Today, however, the paintings of Albert Bierstadt are recognized as one of the treasures of our American artistic heritage.

overleaf: Albert Bierstadt. *Indian Encampment in the Rocky Mountains.* Oil, 48 x 82"

Albert Bierstadt. *Deer in Mountain Home.* Oil, 13 x 18⅝''

Albert Bierstadt. *The Last of the Buffalo.*
1888. Oil sketch, 14⅜ x 19″

Albert Bierstadt. *White Horse in Sunset.*
Oil, 11½ x 15½″

Albert Bierstadt. *Sunset on Peak.* Oil, 13½ x 19″

Albert Bierstadt. *Yellowstone Falls.*
1881. Oil, 44 x 30½″

Thomas Moran

Thomas Moran (1837–1926) was born in Bolton, in Lancashire, England. His family came in 1845 to Philadelphia, where the young Moran was apprenticed to a wood engraver. An older brother, Edward, had received some recognition as a marine painter and shared his knowledge with Thomas.

Moran first worked exclusively in watercolor, but began to use oils about 1860. He went to England in 1862, where he studied and copied works by the dean of Royal Academy painters, Joseph M. W. Turner. He went abroad again in 1866, this time traveling to France and Italy to study the old masters. After thus acquiring the appropriate background and credentials, Moran found his own niche in American art.

At the invitation of Professor F. V. Hayden, Moran accompanied a geological survey into the Yellowstone region of northwestern Wyoming in 1871. Making numerous field sketches in pencil and watercolor, he was able to tap the rich resources of subject matter in the still virtually unexplored northern Rocky Mountain region.

Upon his return to the East, he executed a major work, *The Grand Canyon of the Yellowstone*, which Congress purchased and placed on exhibition in the Capitol. The success of this painting decided the direction of his subsequent career.

In 1873 he made another trip into the West, this time into Utah and Arizona, along the Colorado River. *The Grand Chasm of the Colorado* was the most significant work resulting from this trip. It too was purchased by Congress and was hung with the Yellowstone canvas in the Capital.

Making a trip to the Grand Tetons in 1879, Moran took along a younger brother, Peter, who was gaining a creditable reputation as a painter of wildlife and landscape. All of Moran's energies were devoted to painting the spectacular aspects of the Western landscape.

Though Moran did most of his work in a Long Island studio, he returned regularly to the West for inspiration. He was elected to the National Academy of Design in 1884 and was also a member of the Pennsylvania Academy of the Fine Arts.

Toward the end of his remarkable career he moved to Santa Barbara, California. He made his last journey into the Yellowstone country at the age of eighty-seven and shortly thereafter produced *Mist in the Yellowstone*, a major work that is every bit as fresh and exciting as those resulting from his first trip, fifty-three years earlier.

Thomas Moran stated his purpose in art clearly: "... being true to our own country, in the interpretation of that beautiful and glorious scenery with which Nature has so lavishly endowed our land."

But Moran was an artist first and a natural historian only incidentally. "I place no value on literal transcripts from Nature. My general scope is not realistic; all my tendencies are toward idealization. Of course, all art must come through Nature... but I believe that a place, as a place, has no value in itself for the artist—only so far as it furnishes the material from which to construct a picture."

Thomas Moran. *Golden Gateway to the Yellowstone.*
1893. Oil, 35 x 50″

Thomas Moran. *The Grand Canyon of the Yellowstone.* 1876. Chromolithograph, 9¾ x 14″

Thomas Moran. *Yellowstone Lake.* 1874. Chromolithograph, 9¾ x 14″

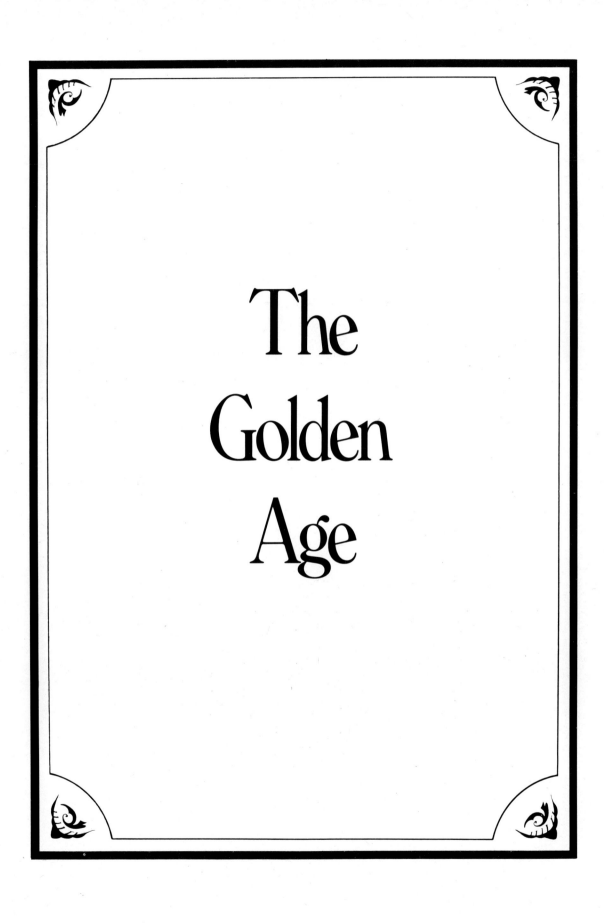

The Golden Age

Charles Schreyvogel. Detail of *How Kola*. 1901. Oil, 26 x 34" *(foldout)*

MIDWAY THROUGH the nineteenth century the character of the West was dramatically altered. The opening of the Oregon Trail in 1844 and the discovery of gold in California four years later brought a deluge of immigrants across the prairies and mountains. Within twenty years the transcontinental railroad was completed, bringing an ever-increasing number of people beyond the Mississippi.

The Western country was unalterably affected by this intrusion, as was the art that reflected this time and this place. The years between the end of the Civil War and the turn of the century were the golden age of the West. The most exciting chapters of the Western pageant—the Indian Wars, the mining booms, the Pony Express, the covered wagons, and the open-range cattle industry—were condensed into this period.

It was also a golden age for the art of the West. The intense drama of the opening of the West provided an unparalleled variety of subjects to challenge the adventurous artist. Two men whose names are practically synonymous with Western art were first-hand observers of this colorful period of our national development. The art of Frederic Remington and Charles M. Russell represents the zenith of this sector of American painting. An essential fact about this era was that art was being produced by men who were on intimate terms with their subject matter.

The style of Western art during the period reflected the general diversification of American painting. Such painters as H. H. Cross, Edgar Paxson, Olaf Seltzer, and to some extent even Russell, were inclined to Romantic sentimentality in their work. But

Charles M. Russell. *Bringing Home the Spoils.* 1909. Oil, 15⅛ x 27¼". The William E. Weiss, Jr., Collection in the Whitney Gallery of Western Art

there was a new Realism in painting, too, involving a rejection of Romantic idealism and the artificialities of Neoclassicism.

The new Realism first achieved wide recognition through the work of Thomas Eakins. Within the framework of Western art, Frederic Remington carried the banner of the new Realism, and he bore it proudly.

After the Civil War, fine art became a special indulgence for the newly wealthy railroad and industrial giants. These men looked to Europe for their art at a time when art on the Continent reflected the influences of the Barbizon School in France and Jean François Millet's sentimental and pious genre paintings. As a result of the successes of Impressionism in the galleries, Western artists were forced to become illustrators in order to make a living.

Time, however, has restored their reputation. Among the most highly regarded American artworks today are paintings produced by men who preferred the prairie and open sky of the West to the salons and tea parties of the East.

Charles M. Russell

Charles M. Russell. *Self-Portrait.* 1900. Watercolor, 13 x 7½"

Charles Marion Russell (1864–1926) is an outstanding Western painter whose work has come to be considered as much a part of the story of the cowboy as roundups and stampedes. Born in Oak Hill, Missouri, of a prominent St. Louis family, young Russell proved to be something of a disappointment to his family. He did not do well in school, and when he was sixteen his parents finally agreed to let him go West, hoping frontier hardships would have a sobering effect.

Arriving in Montana Territory during the boom of the open-range cattle industry, Russell found the country of which he was to be a part for the rest of his life. For the next eleven years, "Kid" Russell, as he was known to his cowboy friends, made his living as a working cowhand. In addition to time spent singing to the horses and cattle, Russell, to the delight of his partners, sketched and painted the men and incidents that filled his daily life on the range.

During the winter of 1888–89, Russell lived in the lodges of the Blood Indians in Canada. Here he learned the intimacies of Indian life, which were not usually known to white men of the day. Many of his most accomplished paintings are of the life of the red man. Russell developed a sympathy and affection for the Indian that was uncharacteristic of white men during this period of continuous friction between the two peoples.

Shortly after his Canadian sojourn, Russell began to seriously consider a career in art; by 1893 he had given up the life of a cowboy for that of an artist. Following his marriage to Nancy Cooper in 1896, and the establishment of a studio at Great Falls, Montana, his reputation evolved steadily from that of the locally popular "cowboy artist" to that of the accomplished painter exhibiting in well-known New York galleries and at the Dore Galleries and the Anglo-American Exposition in London.

Although self-taught, Russell had a many-faceted talent. He became equally skilled at drawing, painting, and sculpture. With respect to technique, he had a firm foundation in drawing and matured in watercolor earlier than in oils. His eventual success as an oil painter stemmed partly from his association with other established artists, beginning with his first visit to New York in 1903. An examination of oil paintings done before and after this period shows an increasing mastery of color and ability to handle more and more difficult problems in composition.

Russell's earlier paintings are solidly drawn, and the muted, subtle colors are those of the prairie. Toward the end of his career, his palette became more extensive. Color became a primary concern, whereas before it had been the dramatic and action-filled content which occupied him most.

He was admittedly a Romantic, and a sensitive, rather than exaggerated, Romanticism is obvious in his work. Russell's experiences were not so wide or varied as those of Remington. His subject matter became somewhat repetitious and insular toward the end of his life.

Today the art of Charles M. Russell commands a high premium in the marketplace. His mature works in pen-and-ink, watercolor, oil, and bronze form the essential core of any comprehensive collection of Western art. The Whitney Gallery of Western Art has an exceptionally large number of Russell's original works in the collection of William E. Weiss.

Charles M. Russell. *Roundup on the Musselshell.* 1919. Oil, 24 x 36″. The William E. Weiss, Jr., Collection in the Whitney Gallery of Western Art

Charles M. Russell. *Single-handed.* 1912. Oil, 30 x 33″. The William E. Weiss, Jr., Collection in the Whitney Gallery of Western Art ▶

Charles M. Russell. *Return of the Warriors.* 1906.
Watercolor, 12¼ x 16½". The William E. Weiss, Jr.,
Collection in the Whitney Gallery of Western Art

Charles M. Russell. *Where Great Herds Come to
Drink.* 1901. Oil, 30½ x 36½". The William E. Weiss,
Jr., Collection in the Whitney Gallery of Western Art

Charles M. Russell. *Escape.* 1908.
Oil, 17 x 12''. The William E. Weiss, Jr.,
Collection in the Whitney Gallery
of Western Art

Charles M. Russell. *Sioux Torturing a Blackfoot Brave.* 1891. Watercolor, 15¼' x 21". The William E. Weiss, Jr., Collection in the Whitney Gallery of Western Art

Charles M. Russell. *Waiting for a Chinook.* Watercolor, 20 x 29"

Charles M. Russell. *A Wounded Grizzly*. 1906. Watercolor, 16½ x 13½″. The William E. Weiss, Jr., Collection in the Whitney Gallery of Western Art

Charles M. Russell. *When Law Dulls the Edge of Chance.* 1915. Oil, 30 x 48".
The William E. Weiss, Jr., Collection in the Whitney Gallery of Western Art

Charles M. Russell. *Whose Meat?.* 1914. Oil, 30 x 42"

Charles M. Russell. *The Stranglers.* 1920. Oil, 30 x 48''. The William E. Weiss, Jr.,
Collection in the Whitney Gallery of Western Art

Frederic Remington

Frederic Remington. *The Roundup.* Oil, 27 x 40''

Frederic S. Remington (1861–1909) is one of the brightest stars in the galaxy of Western art. He was born in Canton, New York, and grew up in an atmosphere of Eastern grace and gentility. As a child he had a gift for drawing and developed a fascination with the Wild West. Young Remington attended a fashionable prep school and entered Yale in 1878. At Yale he distinguished himself in football and boxing, but could not abide academic art instruction.

In 1880, following the death of his father and the acquisition of a comfortable inheritance, Remington left Yale and became a vagabond artist on horseback, roaming throughout the West from Texas to Montana. During this time he became determined to seek a career in art. He bought a small ranch in Kansas in 1883, and by 1886 had become a successful illustrator for the leading magazines of the day. The rest of his life was spent wandering to and from the frontier, pictorially recording an era that was so soon to vanish, as civilization moved westward.

Remington's artistic credo was Realism. In *The History of American Painting,* published in 1905, Samuel Isham said of Remington: "He at least, cannot be said to have sacrificed truth to grace. The raw, crude light, the burning sand, the pitiless blue sky surround the lank sunburned men who ride rough horses and fight and drink or herd cattle as the case may be." Remington painted things as they were, and the historical details in his paintings were carefully researched.

From the late 1880s until his death Remington was the recognized authority on historical authenticity in connection with the West, and the most successful Western artist. As his reputation as an illustrator grew, he began to seek acceptance in fine-art circles. Acceptance came in 1887, when his work was placed on exhibition at the National Academy of Design and the American Water Color Society. In the following years he continued to be successful in the fields of both illustration and easel painting.

In 1889 he received a silver medal at the Paris Exposition and also entered the literary field, writing on Western subjects. He was elected an associate member of the National Academy of Design in 1891 and traveled in Europe and Africa the following year. A one-man exhibition of his work was held in New York in 1893, the first of many such shows which were to highlight his career. Two years later he began to work in sculpture, producing the first and most popular of his pieces, *The Bronco Buster.* His work had begun to be recognized internationally and was exhibited on several occasions at the Royal Academy in London, as well as regularly at the National Academy of Design in New York.

By the time of his last one-man exhibition, held in 1909 at M. Knoedler & Co. in New York, Remington had achieved what he had so long sought. Critical reviews of the last exhibition recognized his efforts on the high level for which he had intended them. One review had this to say: "It must be extremely trying for those commentators on pictorial art who always insisted this distinguished artist was 'only an illustrator,' and decried his ability to paint, to visit such an exhibition as the present one. For by this time, they must be impressed with the fact that Remington's work is splendid in its technique, epic in its imaginative qualities, and historically important in its prominent contributions to the records of the most romantic epoch in the making of the West."

Writing in his diary, the contented artist said, "The critics have all 'come down.' ...

Fredeic Remington. *Hiding the Trail.* Oil, 27 x 40″. The William F. Cody Collection in the Whitney Gallery of Western Art

They ungrudgingly give me a high place as a 'mere painter.' I have been on their trail a long while and they never surrendered while they had a leg to stand on. The 'illustrator' phase has become a background."

The Whitney Gallery of Western Art is distinguished by its individually acquired Remington paintings, as well as by the Frederic Remington Studio Collection, obtained through the W. R. Coe Foundation. This studio collection offers many insights into Remington's artistic genius and constitutes a core of excellence for the entire gallery.

Frederic Remington. *Untitled.* Oil sketch,
15½ x 11¾″

Frederic Remington. *Untitled*. Oil sketch,
25 x 17½″

Frederic Remington. *The Buffalo Hunt.* 1890. Oil.
34 x 49″

Frederic Remington. *The Night Herder*. Oil, 11½ x 17½"

Frederic Remington. *Prospecting for Cattle Range.* 1889. Oil, 29 x 50″

Charles Schreyvogel

Charles Schreyvogel (1861–1912) was a distinguished Western artist at the turn of the century. As a boy in New York, Schreyvogel was apprenticed to an engraver. He received some formal art instruction in Newark and in 1887 went abroad to study in Munich with Karl von Marr and Frank Kirchbach.

After three years he returned to the United States and supported himself through commercial art work. A boyhood fantasy was realized in 1893 when he made his first trip into the West. He spent a summer, primarily in Colorado, sketching and collecting Indian and other frontier relics for studio props.

For the next seven years he continued his commercial art career, at the same time working whenever possible on historical paintings of the Old West. These paintings generally dealt with combat scenes involving the cavalry and the Indians of the Plains. In 1899, surrounded in his Hoboken studio with the weapons and costumes gathered from his Western trips, Schreyvogel produced his most famous painting, *My Bunkie*.

After being rejected for calendar art, *My Bunkie* was submitted halfheartedly to the National Academy of Design for their annual exhibition. It was accepted, and won the principal award, the Thomas B. Clarke prize, in the 1900 competition. This was the turning point in the artist's career. He was elected an associate member of the academy the following year and was able to give up commercial art and concentrate on Western historical painting. After spending the summer of 1900 in the Dakotas, he returned to Hoboken to create popularly acclaimed Indian-warfare pictures.

Schreyvogel continued to produce historical canvases of the West and to make excursions into the field for additional studio props and inspiration. He became interested in sculpture and produced two bronzes, *The Last Drop* and *White Eagle*. A series of forty-eight platinum prints of his paintings were issued in response to his increasing popularity, and thirty-six of his paintings were published in a volume entitled *My Bunkie and Others*.

The Western paintings of Charles Schreyvogel, along with those of Remington and Russell, are considered by many the foundation of any significant institutional collection of Western art.

Charles Schreyvogel. *The Triumph*. 1908. Oil, 20¼ x 16¼"

Charles Schreyvogel. *The Last Drop*. 1903. Bronze, H. 11½"

Charles Schreyvogel. *How Kola.* 1901. Oil, 26 x 34″

Olaf C. Seltzer

Olaf C. Seltzer (1877–1957) was admitted to the Art Institute of his native Copenhagen at the age of twelve. He was able to acquire the fundamentals of drawing and painting through a formal instruction usually afforded only to much older students. In 1892 Seltzer came to the United States to settle in the newly created State of Montana, working as a ranch hand and as a machinist for the railroad.

The impressionable young man spent his spare time along the still-exciting Missouri River, which ran through his home town of Great Falls. Blackfoot Indians, the coming of the railroad, the silver boom, and the open-range cattle industry provided inspiration for a lifetime of painting.

In 1897 Seltzer began to paint in oils. As a result of the growing reputation and the assistance of another Great Falls painter, Charles M. Russell, Seltzer found a ready market for his work.

He moved to New York in 1926 and found an abundance of commissions and financial security. But city life did not appeal to Seltzer, and he returned to Montana the following year. Having made his mark in the East, he continued to receive numerous commissions from Eastern patrons.

His most regular patron was Dr. Philip G. Cole, a Montana native who lived in Tarrytown, New York. Among the Seltzer paintings commissioned by Dr. Cole were over a hundred five-by-six-inch oil paintings depicting Montana historical events. The execution of this project affected the artist's eyesight to the extent that his production in subsequent years was severely curtailed.

Among Seltzer's most highly regarded works are a series of watercolors called "Characters of the Old West," which attest to his intimate knowledge of Western subjects. A superior draftsman, Seltzer was a fine artist in his own right, and it may be unfortunate that he was a home-town contemporary of the more widely known Russell.

Olaf Seltzer enjoyed a very long and artistically productive life. He died in 1957, still very much a painter. Looking back at the dramatic changes he had seen in Montana over the years, he indicated his romantic outlook in a 1932 poem:

> Where are the days of yester years?
> They came, they went; but left no trail,
> No trail like those we dimly see,
> Upon the prairie of today.
> But time will tell, and day by day,
> These trails will slowly fade away,
> As did elusive—yesterday.

above: Olaf C. Seltzer. *The Water Hole.* 1913. Oil, 40 x 60″

below: Olaf C. Seltzer. *Disputed Trail.* 1913. Oil, 31 x 46″

Olaf C. Seltzer. *Watching for White Man's Boat.* Oil, 42 x 53½″

Edgar S. Paxson

Edgar S. Paxson (1852–1919) came to Montana in 1877 from his native New York. With no formal training, Paxson built a career in art on the basis of natural talent and an acute sense of history. Arriving in frontier Montana the winter following Custer's defeat, Paxson was well equipped with the hardiness necessary for life in the still-wild West. He worked at a variety of jobs, each of them characterized by the action and drama of the period and the region. His participation in the events of early Montana history provided him with a rich resource for his career as a Western painter.

Paxson's prominence among Western artists has generally been attributed to the authenticity of the historical details in his paintings. This kind of fidelity has perhaps too often been the criterion for the recognition of many of the arists of the West. Such Paxson paintings as *The Last Shot* reveal considerably greater artistic substance than has generally been realized. At a time when many painters were willing to imitate the strict documentary style which had proven successful, Paxson remained an individual. The refined delicacy with which his background compositions are handled demonstrates that he was concerned with the aesthetic aspects of painting as well as with historical accuracy.

Paxson's monumental paintings, such as *Custer's Last Stand* (his most famous work), and murals in several Montana public buildings account for his success during his lifetime.

Several of Paxson's oil paintings, including *Custer's Last Stand*, are in the collection of the Whitney Gallery of Western Art.

Edgar S. Paxson. *The Buffalo Hunt*. 1905. Oil, 26 x 38¼"

Edgar S. Paxson. Detail of *Custer's Last Stand*. 1889. Oil, 108 x 84"▶

Edgar S. Paxson. *Custer's Last Stand.*
1899. Oil, 84 x 108″

Henry Farny

Henry Farny (1847–1916) demonstrates well the fact that illustrators are capable of producing "fine art."

Farny came to the United States in 1853, at the age of five, from his native Alsace. His family settled in western Pennsylvania, and about 1859 moved to Cincinnati. He began his career as an apprentice with a lithography firm, and by 1865 was doing illustrations for *Harper's Weekly*. The following year he went to Europe to study with Mihály Munkácsy, in Düsseldorf, and with Wilhelm von Diez, in Munich. He spent three and a half years wandering through Germany and Austria, working at any job he could find to pay for art lessons.

In 1870 he returned to Cincinnati and picked up what work he could find in illustration. His accomplishments ranged from circus posters to illustrations for the *McGuffey's Readers*. In 1881 Farny visited the Standing Rock Reservation of the Sioux, which was very much in the news, as Chief Sitting Bull had surrendered there that summer. He found the Indian a compelling subject for art, and decided to concentrate on painting that subject for the rest of his life. In December 1881, shortly after Farny's return from the West, a Cincinnati newspaper reported: "He draws Indians, he paints Indians, he sleeps with an Indian tomahawk near him, he lays greatest store by his Indian necklaces and Indian pipe, he talks Indian and he dreams of Indian warfare." It was about this time that Farny began to paint with an eye toward exhibition rather than illustration.

On a trip to Montana in 1883, he met Sitting Bull and General Ulysses S. Grant. Farny was one of perhaps three artists to sketch the famous Sioux from life.

During the years 1880–90, which were highly successful ones for Farny, his work appeared regularly in the leading periodicals of the day. After 1890 he devoted himself entirely to painting. He visited the West during his period and in 1894 traveled to Fort Sill, Indian Territory, where he was able to sketch the Apache chieftain Geronimo from life.

In spite of his German art training in the Neoclassical style of the Düsseldorf Academy, Farny was a Realist. He was sympathetic, yet not blatantly Romantic, in his attitude toward his subjects. There is a clarity and simplicity in Farny's art that sets it well above showy displays of technique at the expense of communication. His reputation as a painter has steadily increased, and will doubtless continue to do so with the passage of time.

Henry Farny. *Days of Long Ago.* 1903.
Oil, 36 x 22''

Joseph H. Sharp

Joseph H. Sharp. *White Swan—Crow.* c. 1903. Oil, 17½ x 11¾″

Joseph Henry Sharp (1859–1953) was born in Bridgeport, Ohio, and began studying art at the McMicken School of Design in Cincinnati at the age of fourteen. Later, while a student at the Cincinnati Art Academy, he and the young Ohio artist Henry Farny became fast friends. Recalling his art-student days, Sharp wrote: "I was first interested in Indians before becoming an artist . . . . When I went to Cincinnati Art Academy and learned to draw and paint, I wanted to paint Indians—Farny was doing it then, and dissuaded me by telling of hardships, dangers . . . after a couple of years or so when he saw I was determined to go west, he gave me books on Pueblo Indians."

In 1881 Sharp went to Antwerp to study with Charles Verlat. Later he studied in Munich with Karl Marr, and in Paris with Jean-Paul Laurens and Benjamin Constant. In the summer of 1883 he made his first visit to Santa Fe, New Mexico. Subsequent summers were spent touring Italy and Spain.

In 1892 Sharp accepted an instructorship at the Cincinnati Art Academy. The following summer he saw Taos, New Mexico, for the first time. Visiting at the Académie Julian in Paris that same year, Sharp recounted his impressions of Taos to students Bert Phillips and Ernest Blumenshein. His vivid descriptions of the landscape and Indians of the village led to the founding of the area's school of Western painting. Phillips was the first of the three men to settle permanently in Taos (1898), and is thus considered the founder of the Taos colony, which attracted other fine painters like Oscar Berninghaus, Walter Ufer, and E. Irving Couse.

In 1901 Sharp opened a summer studio on the Crow Reservation in Montana. The following year he gave up his teaching position in Cincinnati so that he could devote himself to painting. In 1912 he became a permanent resident of Taos.

Sharp was primarily a painter of Indian portraits. Eleven of his efforts in this category were purchased by the Smithsonian in 1900. He also executed many fine genre pieces, usually done among northern Indians, which indicate a studied approach to the problems of perspective, and of light and shadow. Sharp was somewhat deaf, but this handicap did not dampen his artistic enthusiasm. His sympathy for and understanding of the Indian accounts for the warmth and vitality in the best of his paintings.

opposite page, left: Joseph H. Sharp. *Tom and Jerry—Drummers.* Oil, 23 x 17″

opposite page, right: Joseph H. Sharp. *Crow Reservation Study.* Oil, 11¾ x 5½″

Joseph H. Sharp. *The Crow
War Bonnet.* Oil, 24 x 20"

Joseph H. Sharp. *Dividing the Chief's Property.* Oil, 30 x 40″

Joseph H. Sharp. *Crow Reservation.* Oil, 11¾ x 17¾″

Joseph H. Sharp. *Burial Cortege of a Crow Chief.* Oil, 30 x 40"

Henry H. Cross

Henry H. Cross (1837–1918) was an adventurous youth who, in the tradition of the children's story of Toby Tyler, ran away from his New York home to join the circus. His life came to be closely tied to the big top. He developed his talent as an artist by painting wild animals on the sides of the circus wagons for such shows as that of P. T. Barnum.

When Cross was sixteen, he followed the sawdust trail to Europe. In Paris he attracted the attention of Rosa Bonheur, the outstanding European painter of animals. She helped the young Cross by offering art instruction, and together they delighted in visiting horse shows and rural fairs throughout the French countryside.

Cross had a childlike fascination for the West. Upon his return to the United States in 1860, he settled in Chicago and began to do portraits on commission. Two years later he enthusiastically headed for southwestern Minnesota, where there was a Sioux uprising. The real West impressed him even more than the Wild West shows he had known for so long.

For years after this first frontier experience, Cross often made trips in the West, frequently traveling alone at a time when it was dangerous to do so. His enthusiasm and good nature made him a welcome guest wherever he visited, and afforded him enviable opportunities to have many Western notables, both white men and Indians, pose for his portraits.

Cross's portraiture, particularly that of Indian chiefs, is his best work. However, he also executed many genre pieces, among them what is perhaps his most widely known piece, *The Victor*, which was purchased by William F. Cody. This painting, along with other examples of the artist's work, is included in the collection of the Whitney Gallery of Western Art.

Henry H. Cross. *The Moose Hunter.*
Oil, 30 x 24"

Henry H. Cross. *The Victor.* 1878. Oil, 95 x 71"

The
Fading Frontier

Edward Borein. Detail of *Crow Medicine Man.*
Watercolor, 6½ x 9″ *(foldout)*

In 1927, the noted art historian Samuel Isham stated: "In the development of early art, Western art enjoyed universal acclaim and a truly distinguished position in the body of American art. Somewhere along the line, near the turn of the century and as the influences of French impressionism began to exert themselves, Western art fell into critical disfavor, although there was no essential departure from the established patterns of this segment of American painting."

It was as if with the closing of the frontier and the permanent settlement of the West, the art of the region no longer held the fascination it once had. There were certainly accomplished artists still painting Western subjects, but they were no longer accorded an honored position in the arts.

At the bottom of this curious turn of events lay factors that altered the very foundations of American painting. American art at the turn of the present century was in a period of transition. There was no single established American pattern. There were artists, critics, and patrons for a diverse spectrum of painting styles which encompassed everything from Neoclassicism to French Impressionism. Then, what had begun as a healthy reaction to Victorian decorum by "The Eight" painters who introduced the "Ash Can" school of realism into the mainstream of American art gradually resulted in the negation of representational art principles.

The artists who found their inspiration and subjects in the West were left out of the new mainstream. Ambiguity in art became the vogue, while painters of the West remained true to styles which reflected commonly held concepts of reality. As a result, many of the artists who are represented in this section did not receive critical acceptance during their careers.

The Western art produced since the turn of this century has recently moved back from relative obscurity to critical acceptance. We are fortunate that twentieth-century Western painters kept alive important art values during a period when it would have been much easier to give in to the destructiveness of modernism. Today, they continue to paint a land and a people that are every bit as worthy of artistic attention as were the mountain men and the Green River Valley when Alfred Jacob Miller first saw them in 1837. If the contemporary countryside of France and Italy have sustaining relevance in fine art, so too have the prairies and mountains of the fading frontier.

William R. Leigh

William R. Leigh (1866–1955) was born on a farm in West Virginia. At the age of twelve he received an award of one hundred dollars for one of his animal drawings from the well-known Washington patron W.W. Corcoran. As a young man, Leigh spent three years at the Maryland Institute of Art in Baltimore and then received further training at the Royal Academy in Munich.

Returning from Germany in 1896, Leigh became involved in the New York illustrating fraternity and within a year was undertaking field assignments for *Scribner's Magazine*. He made his first trip West, to North Dakota, in 1897. Here he found the subject matter most interesting to him as an artist: "From the moment I returned from my studies in Europe, I had wanted to go West, which I had already determined was the really true America, and what I wanted to paint."

In 1906 he traveled to New Mexico and decided to quit the illustration field and devote himself to more serious painting. Visits to the West became more frequent: "My interest in the West began long before I can remember. I found it all and more than I had dared to expect or hope, and I believe it has called forth the best there is in me."

A vast collection of sketches, notes, and studies found in Leigh's studio at the time of his death attests to the seriousness of purpose with which he approached painting. His German training had instilled in Leigh the importance of extensive preliminary work prior to the execution of a finished painting; furthermore, some of his canvases were enormous in scope. He was an accomplished painter in both the aesthetic and the technical senses. Eugen Neuhaus, in his *History and Ideals of American Art*, says, "His pictures have the sophistication and finesse of the schooled painter."

By 1920 Leigh was established as among the best painters of the West. Exhibitions in important galleries were as frequent as the winning of medals and other awards. He was elected a member of the National Academy of Design in 1955. Nine days after he received this honor, he died in New York, his reputation intact. His *Buffalo Drive* is one of the most popular pieces in the collection of the Whitney Gallery of Western Art.

William R. Leigh. *Wounded Grizzly.* 1915. Oil, 24 x 36″. Mr. and Mrs. Nedward Frost
Collection in the Whitney Gallery of Western Art

William R. Leigh. *The Buffalo Drive*. 1947.
Oil, 6′ 6″ x 10′ 6″

Edward Borein

Edward Borein. *Holding Up the Stage.* Watercolor,
9½ x 14⅝″

Edward Borein (1873-1945) grew up in the ranch country of California. By the time he was twenty he had established himself as a good *vaquero* for the Jesus Maria Rancho at Santa Maria, and had also begun to take his sketching hobby seriously. As a young man Borein was something of a saddle vagabond and itinerant artist. He rode horseback throughout the Western range country, sketching in Oregon, Montana, Wyoming, Canada, and the Southwest. He could always get a job as a cowhand when he ran out of money.

In 1907 Borein made the decision to commit himself to a career in art. He had had reasonable success in finding a market for his work in Western publications at a time when the competition was stiff. Wanting professional instruction, he moved to New York and attended the Art Students League, whereupon his work greatly improved. He became a central figure in the colony of Western painters and illustrators who lived in the city. Borein's Forty-second street studio was Charlie Russell's favorite hangout. Here Borein also became friends with Will Rogers, James Swinnerton, Frank Tenney Johnson, Joe DeYong, and other prominent men who shared his affection for the West.

When Borein ultimately returned to California, he opened a studio in Santa Barbara. He became an accomplished etcher, did innumerable pen and ink drawings, and gained the reputation of being among the best watercolorists in the Western field. He also worked in oils, but not with the mastery he evidenced in other mediums.

His devotion to the West was more than just an affinity to a particular regional subject matter. He was a deep-dyed Westerner and would have been so had he never painted. Many artists have been born in the West, but it is a rather sad fact that the best have generally come from the East or Europe. Even Russell and Remington were from non-western cities, the one from St. Louis and the other from New York. Borein is one of the very few outstanding Western artists who had their roots naturally implanted in the Western soil, and his works are today among the most avidly sought after in the field of Western art.

Edward Borein. *Crow Medicine Man.* Watercolor, 6½ x 9″ ▶

W. Herbert Dunton

W. Herbert (Buck) Dunton (1878-1936) was born in Augusta, Maine. He achieved his initial artistic success as a Western fiction illustrator at about the same time as did the illustrator Frank Tenney Johnson, and like Johnson he went on to a career in painting. Dunton attended the New York Art Students League, where he was taught by Ernest Blumenschein. Blumenschein was a founder of the Taos art colony, and he encouraged Dunton to move to New Mexico and become the sixth of the original founders of the Taos Art Society.

Moving West in 1912, Dunton was able to adapt his Eastern training to Western subject matter and to produce paintings that had an appeal beyond that of regionalism. Painting with such artists as Blumenschein, Couse, Berninghaus, Ufer, and Sharp helped develop Dunton's technique and intensify his dedication to aesthetic goals.

Dunton found in the Southwest the ideal combination of light and color and of Indian and Mexican life for his paintings. In 1922 he wrote of the Southwest in the *American Magazine of Art:* ". . . the skies of marvelous blue through which pass, in summer, regiments of stately clouds; the majesty of the mountains, those serrated, rugged peaks to the East and North, and the gentler tones of the remoter ranges low lying in the West. . . . Every turn unfolds a new wonderland of beauty. The timbered sides of the mountains capped in snow are now carpeted in the delicate pattern of the changes, aspens, gold and russet against the green of the pines. The heat of summer is gone. . . . Everywhere the sage, the adobes and the cottonwoods melt together in one harmonious symphony of greys and browns and violets of the choicest quality."

It was indeed the proper environment for this artist. He later wrote: "I have found the secret of contentment, which is in the work you love and the enjoyment of the simple things." He spent long periods in the desert and the mountains and came to know the land intimately. Dunton died on March 18, 1936. One critic has said of his work: "His paintings have a notable realism which, when combined with his talent for decorative feeling, gives his canvases a striking and modern effect."

W. Herbert Dunton. *The Custer Fight.* Oil, 32 x 50″

Frank Tenney Johnson

Frank Tenney Johnson (1874-1939) was born on an Iowa farm at a time when the frontier influence was still very much alive. Iowa settlements in the closing decades of the nineteenth century were ports on the shores of the prairie seas. As the final groups of pioneer wagons moved through Iowa and out across the Great Plains, the romance of those days left its impression deeply stamped upon the mind of the young boy.

Johnson went to New York in 1902 and became a student of Robert Henri at the Art Students League. In 1904 he made a six-month sketching trip into the West, spending an eventful summer in Colorado ranch country. He found quick acceptance as an illustrator for leading Western authors of the day, and in later years he frequently returned to the West to sketch and to observe.

The money he earned from illustrating enabled Johnson to concentrate on easel painting. In New York he became a close friend of the cartoonist and illustrator Clyde Forsythe. Forsythe, a native Californian, induced Johnson to move to California. The two friends shared a studio in Alhambra for many years, and were the founders of the Biltmore Gallery in Los Angeles.

Johnson was a meticulous painter. He developed a technique for depicting nocturnal Western scenes which has not been duplicated to this day. His work was accomplished through continual study and effort, and had the distinctiveness characteristic of all great painters. He always retained his close affinity with the West, maintaining a summer studio near Cody, Wyoming, up to the time of his death.

His devotion to Western subjects was as unwavering as his dedication to excellence in painting. Indian and Mexican life in the Southwest, and the range cattle industry of Wyoming and Colorado were Johnson's favorite subjects. His paintings, which are generally tranquil rather than dramatic, evidence a mastery of color unusual in the field of Western art.

He was elected to the Salmagundi Club, the National Arts Club, and the National Academy of Design.

Frank Tenney Johnson. *On the Moonlit Trail.* 1938. Oil, 16 x 12"

W. H. D. Koerner

W. H. D. Koerner (1878-1938) was a German-born illustrator who became closely associated with some of the landmarks of Western literature. His illustrations for the works of such authors as Emerson Hough and Eugene Manlove Rhodes gave Koerner the public exposure that was vital to his career.

Koerner grew up on the fringe of the frontier in Iowa during the 1880s and nineties. He first worked professionally as an illustrator for the *Chicago Tribune*. While in Chicago he attended the Chicago Art Institute and the Francis Smith Art Academy. He began to do free-lance commercial illustrating while pursuing more serious painting in his spare time. About 1905 he went to New York for further study and a chance at a more lucrative career. He studied under George Bridgman at the Art Students League, and by 1907 his work was good enough to gain him entry into the privileged circle of the students of Howard Pyle.

With fellow students N. C. Wyeth, Harvey Dunn, Frank Schoonover, and Anton Otto Fischer, Koerner learned from Pyle during intense critical sessions at Pyle's home in Wilmington, Delaware. Koerner's work for a time showed the unmistakable influence of Pyle's teaching. During the 1920s, however, the artist spent several summers studying the new technique of "broken color" with its pioneer, Frank Breckenridge. It was this experience which led to the development of a personal style of painting.

"Broken color" painting utilizes a full palette of rainbow colors, omitting black and brown, and is much more suited to fine art than to commercial illustration. By perfecting this technique Koerner was able to transcend the label of "mere illustrator" and to merit attention as a serious painter. He began to paint more subjectively and aggressively, with conviction evident in each brushstroke.

His work became familiar to millions through his long association with the *Saturday Evening Post*. Today his canvases are recognized for their fine aesthetic and technical qualities. Koerner's work also has great popular appeal, the basis of which lies in the artist's depiction of intriguing character and individuality in each of his subjects. About the only autobiographical comment attributable to Koerner is: "Never could write, never could talk. . . . Look over the bunch of illustrations I've done, and you'll see my life, feel the struggles I've felt, know my joys and sorrows."

opposite page, above: W. H. D. Koerner. *Moving the Herd.* 1923. Oil, 26¼ x 56"

opposite page, below: W. H. D. Koerner. *Trail Herd to Wyoming.* 1932. Oil, 22 x 72"

W. H. D. Koerner. *Unwelcome Intruders*. 1932.
Oil, 28 x 40″

N.C. Wyeth

Newell Convers Wyeth (1882–1945) is the patriarch of one of America's most artistic dynasties. He was born in Needham, Massachusetts, attended Pape's Art School in Boston, and, after some additional instruction, found his niche as one of Howard Pyle's special "group of seven" at Wilmington, Delaware.

Wyeth came under Pyle's influence to such an extent that it was difficult for him to develop an artistic identity distinct from that of his mentor. *Scribner's Magazine* commented in 1906: "Mr. Wyeth is another one of the group included among Mr. Pyle's pupils and this statement is always a guarantee of at least a seriousness of intent and conscientious application toward a distinct art ideal."

Along with Harvey Dunn, Wyeth became one of the best known of Pyle's many pupils. He was among the most successful illustrators during a period when illustrating was enjoying a golden age in the United States. The books for which he did illustrations ranged from children's classics such as *Treasure Island, The Song of Hiawatha,* and *Robin Hood* to such important Western works as *The Oregon Trail, Jinglebob, Ramona,* and *Arizona Nights.*

In later years Wyeth began to paint more for exhibition. His prominence as an illustrator allowed him to be selective in accepting commissions. Besides producing many paintings, he executed murals for the Reading Public Museum and Art Gallery in Pennsylvania, the Missouri State Capitol, the Boston Federal Reserve Bank, and the New York Public Library.

As a result of long practice as an art teacher, and through experimentation in mediums other than oil, such an egg tempera, Wyeth went beyond illustration. Eventually he began to do dramatic paintings of historical subjects. Wyeth, a robust and spirited man, had a particular affinity for the West. Among his many fine canvases of Western life are a series of outstanding oils done as a result of a visit to Colorado ranches in 1904. They not only evidence the young Wyeth's attention to authentic detail, they also demonstrate a masterful handling of perspective and composition.

N. C. Wyeth's emergence as an easel painter was not widely recognized at the time of his accidental death in 1945. Such recognition, however, has come with time. Wyeth's contributions as a painter and as a teacher are widely respected today.

N. C. Wyeth. *In the Corral.* 1904. Oil, 38 x 26″. The John M. Schiff Collection in the Whitney Gallery of Western Art

N. C. Wyeth. *Cutting Out.* 1904. Oil, 38 x 26″. The John M. Schiff Collection in the Whitney Gallery of Western Art

Winold Reiss

Winold Reiss (1888-1953) made a career of painting portraits of the Blackfoot Indians of Montana. The German-born Reiss studied art under his father, a landscape painter, and later attended the Royal Academy in Munich. He grew up in Europe at a time when the American West was all the rage on the Continent. Through countless pulp magazines and the tours of such Western notables as William F. Cody, German boys were as addicted to cowboys and Indians as were American youngsters.

Reiss became determined to go to America and see the Indians very early in life. He managed the voyage to New York in 1913 but found that it was still a long way to Indian country. In 1919 Reiss was finally able to go West. He visited the little town of Browning, on the Montana Blackfoot reservation, and finally found what he had sought since leaving Germany. Reiss returned often to Browning to paint the Blackfeet. It became his life's work.

He was a prolific painter, producing as many as seventy-five portraits in a summer at Browning. For many years he taught art at New York University during the school term and painted and taught in Montana in the summers.

He was a literalist in depicting members of the Blackfoot tribe. His portraits are marked by a strict fidelity to the physical appearance of subjects and to their various and colorful costumes. Especially distinctive is his mastery of composition and color. Reiss was able, through background and the depiction of his subject's costume and other personal articles, to create something infinitely more interesting, both artistically and ethnologically, than just an Indian portrait.

Reiss's contribution to Western art is along the same lines as that of George Catlin. Reiss concurred with Catlin's statement that "the history and customs of such a people, preserved by pictorial illustrations, are themes worthy of the lifetime of one man." Reiss had the chance to paint the last generation of Northern Plains Indians who could still recall running buffalo and doing honorable battle with red and white enemies. At his death, Reiss's ashes were appropriately scattered by his Blackfoot friends along a stream at the edge of the Rockies, on the reservation where he had felt at home.

Winold Reiss. *The Sign Talkers*. Watercolor and pastel, 52 x 30"

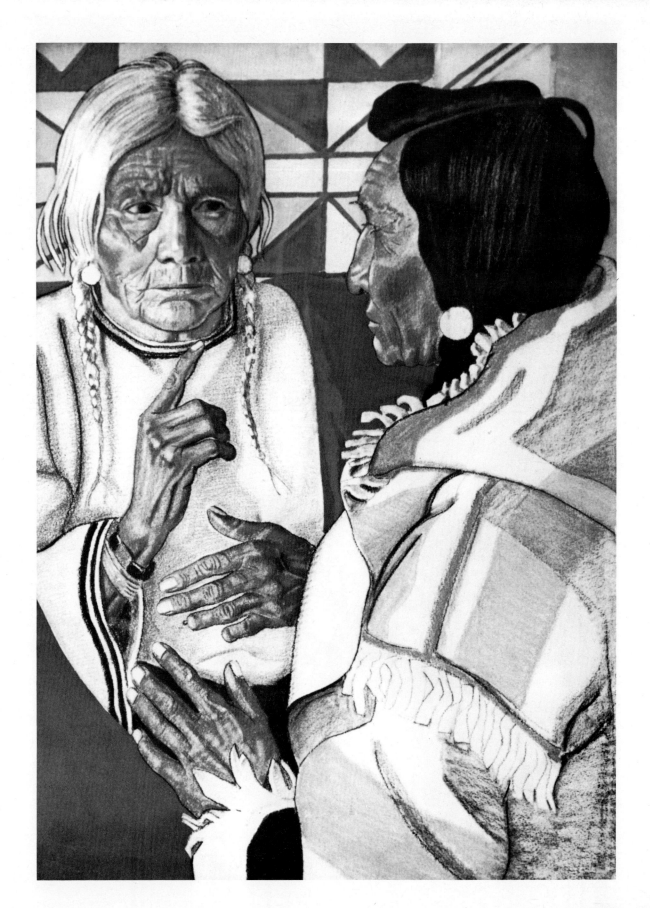

Winold Reiss. *Brave and Squaw*. Watercolor and pastel, 30 x 22"

Winold Reiss. *Bear Head.* Watercolor
and pastel, 30 x 22"

Carl Rungius

Carl Rungius (1869-1959) was German-born and received formal art training in Berlin, attending the Berlin School of Art, the Academy of Fine Arts, and the School of Applied Arts. Rungius's grandfather was a taxidermist and animal painter, and his father, a minister, was deeply interested in wildlife conservation. It was therefore natural that Carl should want to paint wildlife.

In 1894 the young German artist came to America as a guest of an uncle in New York. The following year, at the Sportsman's Show in New York City, Rungius met Ira Dodge, a hunting guide from Wyoming. The resulting trip West decided the course of the artist's life. He was both a painter and a hunter, and in the mountains of Wyoming he found abundant satisfaction in both pursuits.

After returning to Germany for a year, Rungius came back to the United States for good. For the rest of his life his art was fostered by yearly sketching and hunting trips to Wyoming, New Brunswick, and Alberta. He maintained a studio, first on Long Island, and then, from 1910 until his death, in New York City.

During his first years in America he did illustrations for the popular magazines of the day, but by about 1904 he was concentrating full time on painting for exhibition. In 1913 he was elected an associate member of the National Academy of Design, and he became a full member in 1920.

From 1921 until his death Rungius maintained a summer studio at Banff, in Alberta, Canada. The majority of his paintings are of North American big-game animals, but he also did several canvases of cowboy and hunting-party scenes. The landscapes in his work are as significant as the primary figures of animals or men.

Rungius's work attracted the attention of such men as Theodore Roosevelt and Frederic Remington. A visit to Rungius's studio in 1908 prompted Remington to comment in a letter: "I am going into a farm proposition up in Connecticut which is to be my 'last stand,' and it keeps me hard up; but as soon as I get settled I mean to own a Rungius. . . . I think records of us fellows who are doing the 'Old America' which is so fast passing will have an audience in posterity."

Carl Rungius. *Wyoming Antelope.* Oil, 30 x 40″

Carl Rungius. *Wyoming Elk.* Oil, 30 x 40″

Nick Eggenhofer

Nick Eggenhofer (born 1897) is one of the most prolific of all the artists who have used Western subject matter. He has produced about thirty thousand sketches, drawings, and paintings. The majority of his efforts have appeared as illustrations in magazines and books.

Eggenhofer was born in Southern Bavaria and came to the United States when he was sixteen. While working as an apprentice at the American Lithograph Company in New York, he attended night classes in art at Cooper Union. His interest in the West goes back to his German boyhood, when William F. Cody's Wild West Show had made a highly successful continental tour. Eggenhofer's initial art efforts had Western subjects, although he had not yet visited the West.

The aspiring artist found a large market for his drawings in the Western pulps of the publishing house of Street and Smith. During the following decades, Eggenhofer visited the West often and continually added to his extensive research files. His signature became well known to the readers of Western stories.

Since moving to Cody, Wyoming, in 1961, Eggenhofer has concentrated on painting. His most effective efforts have been in the medium of gouache, essentially watercolor prepared with a gum binder to give the paint a body and opacity which approaches the quality of oil. Eggenhofer is widely recognized for his accurate depiction of early Western horse-drawn transportation. In 1961 his definitive work on this subject, *Wagons, Mules and Men*, was published. He has also executed several sculptures which have been cast in bronze in recent years.

Eggenhofer does not shun the label of illustrator. In this regard he says: "I have always like to paint pictures that tell a story. There is plenty of room for imagination and creativity. The problems presented in doing a good illustration can be just as challenging artistically as in a painting to hang on a wall."

Nick Eggenhofer. *Wyoming String Team.* 1966. Oil, 32 x 60″

Maynard Dixon

Maynard Dixon (1875-1946) was sixteen when he sent his sketchbook to Frederic Remington for comment. Remington wrote back to encourage Dixon, and in the early 1890s the aspiring painter left the family home in the San Joaquin country of California to pursue painting as a career.

Success as an easel painter did not come quickly. Dixon spent twenty years as a magazine and newspaper illustrator, during which he also executed several murals in California and Arizona. He continued to do murals throughout his career, but several years as a commercial illustrator in New York only strengthened his desire to produce gallery paintings in the West.

About 1920 he left illustrating to others and began to travel extensively throughout the West, sketching as he went. His earliest work from this period focused primarily on color, but as he gained experience, his paintings showed increasing concern with structure. His most characteristic mature works depict Southwestern and California desert landscapes and their inhabitants.

Dixon saw men in the Southwest as integral features of the environment. He was able to successfully communicate this vision in his work, through a subtle blending of desert, sky, and man into a perfect and harmonious whole. Outspoken in his opinions of art, he stated that "there has been more nonsense written about art than any other subject. The proof of all art lies simply in what it can add to the experience of the beholder."

Speaking of "fashionable art" in his day, Dixon said: "Most American painters are stylists and fashion mongers. Few have the authentic vision of the true artist . . . to make art a la mode is to reduce it to the level of millinery . . . a true artist keeps his own integrity. He bewares of cults and dogmas. He learns from all and gives allegiance to none."

Maynard Dixon. *The Medicine Robe.*
1915. Oil, 40 x 30″

John Clymer

John Clymer (born 1907) grew up in Ellensburg, Washington. He studied at the Vancouver School of Art, the Ontario College of Art, the Wilmington Society of Fine Arts, and under Harvey Dunn at the Grand Central School of Art in New York. Clymer's Eastern training was in the "Brandywine tradition" of N. C. Wyeth, and his illustrations have appeared in many leading publications in the United States and Canada, including the *Saturday Evening Post.*

In recent years, Clymer has turned entirely to fine art. His first one-man show was held at the Grand Central Galleries in New York in 1964. He has proved his talent as an easel painter, winning such awards as the oil-painting gold medal in the 1970 exhibition at the Cowboy Hall of Fame in Oklahoma City.

Among the most popular works in the Whitney Gallery of Western Art are three mural-size paintings by Clymer which were commissioned by Winchester-Western Company. These three paintings — *The Cattle Drive, The Gold Train,* and *The Homesteaders* — are highly accomplished works of art and are historically interesting as well.

Clymer moved to Wyoming to live in 1971, after spending many years in Connecticut. He finds his inspiration for painting in an endless variety of Western subjects but is particularly attracted to the individuals and incidents of the early Western fur trade, which he renders with painstaking historical correctness. Of the source of his inspiration, Clymer has said: "I am interested in painting all subjects that relate to the West, past and present. Life in the out-of-doors, on the prairies, or in the mountains is a never-ending source of wonder . . . to me."

John Clymer. *The Cattle Drive.* 1970.
Oil, 120 x 60″

John Clymer. *The Gold Train.* 1970. Oil,
60 x 120″

John Clymer. *The Homesteaders* (detail at right). 1970. Oil, 120 x 60″

The West in Sculpture

THE FIRST distinguishable "American" trend in sculpture came in the nineteenth century, as sculptors developed the themes of Indian and animal life in the West. Many sculptors in the United States, as well as eminent European masters, found the "noble savage" a particularly appealing subject for idealization in bronze.

In fact, sculpture using Western subjects enjoys a broader, less regional reputation than do the paintings of the West. Cyrus Dallin's heroic *Appeal to the Great Spirit* is installed prominently in front of the Museum of Fine Arts in Boston. This artist's rugged sculptures of Western subjects are also displayed in other non-Western cities, such as Hanover and Philadelphia, in Pennsylvania.

Among the outstanding American sculptors of the nineteenth and twentieth centuries were several who were native sons of the West. Classical educations in sculpture at such art meccas as the Académie Julian and the Ecole des Beaux-Arts provided these men with the technical means to convey their impressions of the Western scene.

James Earle Fraser, the creator of a number of America's finest sculptures, was raised on the Dakota prairies. Dallin was born in Utah, as was Solon Borglum, who worked as a cowhand in his youth. Remington and Russell, though both essentially self-taught in the medium of sculpture, equaled, and in some instances even surpassed, their better-known efforts as painters.

The history of the American West is replete with heroic themes and individuals ideally suited to representation in bronze. What has been accomplished thus far is one of the strongest artistic testimonies to patriotism and the American character.

James Earle Fraser

James Earle Fraser (1876–1953) stands near the top of most lists of great American sculptors. He was responsible for what has become the single best-known piece of Western art, regardless of medium. This piece, the heroic sculpture *The End of the Trail,* is admired throughout the world.

Fraser was born in Winona, Minnesota, and grew up in railroad construction camps in the Dakotas. He began to carve animals in chalkstone when he was eight. Fraser always recalled with affection "the prairie that was home to me." His public-school days were spent in Minneapolis and Chicago, where he won several city-wide art competitions. He received instruction from the sculptor Richard Bock while still in his teens and later attended the Chicago Art Institute.

In 1894 Fraser went to Paris to study at the École des Beaux-Arts and the Académie Julian. His first model of *The End of the Trail* won a Paris competition in 1898 and attracted the attention of the eminent Augustus Saint-Gaudens. Young Fraser became Saint-Gaudens's protege and returned to America to assist in several of the famous sculptor's best-known pieces. Among these was the statue of William Tecumseh Sherman that was installed in New York City. The four years spent with Saint-Gaudens were essential to Fraser's development as an artist.

His first important commission came in 1906, through Saint-Gaudens's suggestion that he do the bust of President Theodore Roosevelt for the Senate chamber. From 1906 through 1911 Fraser taught at the New York Art Students League. He was continually offered commissions, developed an interest in creating medals and medallions, and executed heroic sculptures of famous Americans like Daniel Boone and Abraham Lincoln for numerous public buildings and memorials.

Sculptures such as *Buffalo Prayer,* in the Whitney Gallery of Western Art, embody what were to Fraser the ideal symbols of the West. The spirit of this piece and that of *The End of the Trail* are similar. Both reflect Fraser's sympathy for the plight of the Western Indian. Fraser also used the theme of Indian and buffalo in executing the models for the buffalo nickel.

Fraser's accomplishments in the arts were far-reaching in their influence on American culture, and the ideals represented in his sculptured images inspire all who see them.

James Earle Fraser. *Buffalo Prayer*. Bronze, H. 8′ 9″

James Earle Fraser. *The End of the Trail* (detail at left). c. 1918. Bronze, H. 33¾"

Solon H. Borglum

Solon H. Borglum. *Bucky O'Neil.* 1907.
Bronze, H. 41″

Solon H. Borglum (1868-1922) was born in Ogden, Utah, and spent his youth in the Western range country. Borglum's parents had come to America from Denmark and traveled by wagon to Utah. The elder Borglum was a woodcarver, but soon after their fourth child, Solon, was born, he went to St. Louis to study medicine, taking the family with him.

After medical school, Borglum settled his family in Fremont, Nebraska. Solon and his brother Gutzon grew up in the prairie environment, as Arthur Goodrich has put it, "hardy and quick and clear-headed, fit for action and hardship." When Solon was fifteen, he and Gutzon were sent to work on a ranch in California. Solon learned to be a good stockman. He returned to Nebraska to run a ranch for his father and lived the rough life of a cowboy for several years.

In the meantime Gutzon had sought a career in art and encouraged Solon to do the same, although Solon had thus far shown no inclination in this direction. He began, however, to sketch during the winter seasons on the Nebraska ranch. In 1893 he left the ranch and became an itinerant painter, finally opening a studio in Santa Ana, California.

Hard times in California convinced him of his need for training. He moved east and entered the Cincinnati Art Academy. At the academy he began to develop an interest in sculpture, a medium which, he found, suited him much more than painting. His models won academy competitions and a scholarship. Through the efforts of his teacher, Louis T. Rebisso, he was able to go to Paris to study.

In Paris he studied alone in the galleries and museums. He received encouragement and advice from the French sculptors Emmanuel Frémiet and Denys Puech, and "a few words of approval" from Augustus Saint-Gaudens. He spent a short time at the Académie Julian and in 1898 and 1899 exhibited medal-winning pieces in the Paris Salon.

Borglum returned to America in 1899. His work won medals at the Paris Exposition in 1900, at the Pan American Exposition in Buffalo in 1901, and at the St. Louis Exposition in 1904. He established a studio at Silvermine, Connecticut, and subsequently founded the American School of Sculpture in New York City. Borglum was elected an associate member of the National Academy of Design in 1911. The New York critic Charles H. Caffin found his work to be "fresh in its inspiration, large in feeling; poignant in repose, or vigorous without exaggeration. Moreover, it is unmistakably American. It has grown out of the peculiar experiences of American conditions and partakes of that large freedom whence it originated."

Solon H. Borglum. *Night Hawking.* 1898. Bronze, H. 13″

Solon H. Borglum. *One in a Thousand.*
c. 1906. Bronze, H. 41¾"

Cyrus E. Dallin

Cyrus E. Dallin (1861-1944) executed one of the two most widely known of Western sculptures. A heroic bronze casting of his *Appeal to the Great Spirit* is installed in front of the Museum of Fine Arts in Boston. Smaller versions of this same piece are in numerous collections, and countless copies exist both in sculpture and prints. *Appeal to the Great Spirit*, like James Earle Fraser's *The End of the Trail*, is on display in the Whitney Gallery of Western Art.

Cyrus Dallin was born in Springville, Utah. He went to Europe for study in 1889 and attended classes at both the École des Beaux-Arts and the Académie Julian. He was a student of Henri-Michel Chapu, and also worked with the painter Rosa Bonheur during the time when William F. Cody's Wild West Show was in Paris.

Dallin enjoyed a distinguished career as a sculptor. He won gold medals in competitions of the American Art Association in 1888, of the Chicago Exposition in 1893, and of the San Francisco Exposition of 1915. His work won a silver medal at the Paris Exposition of 1900. He was a member of the National Academy of Design, and of such elite groups as the Royal Society of Arts in London and the American Academy of Arts and Letters. Dallin was also a teacher and a writer.

In addition to *Appeal to the Great Spirit*, he modeled several other heroic pieces. Among these are: *The Signal of Peace*, in Lincoln Park, Chicago; the statue of Massasoit, in Plymouth, Massachusetts; *The Cavalryman*, in Hanover, Pennsylvania; and *The Medicine Man*, in Fairmount Park in Philadelphia. All these large pieces and most of his smaller works are concerned with Classical interpretations of Western subjects. Dallin was particularly intrigued with the Indian, and his Indian-equestrian pieces, such as *Appeal to the Great Spirit* and *The Medicine Man*, are considered his finest works.

Cyrus E. Dallin. *Appeal to the Great Spirit* (two views).
1913. Bronze, H. 21⅛″

Alexander Phimister Proctor

Alexander Phimister Proctor (1862-1950) was born in Bozanquit, Ontario, the fourth child of a hardy pioneering family of eleven children. He spent most of his youth in Iowa and Colorado, hunting, trapping, fishing, and enjoying the frontier experience.

His father encouraged his artistic interest. The young Proctor took lessons in Denver and began to learn the process of wood engraving. In 1885 he went East to study in New York. Proctor enrolled at the National Academy of Design and spent two winters at the Art Students League, but he returned to the West each summer to sketch and enjoy nature.

During the fall and winter of 1887 he became acquainted with the sculptor John Rogers and began to take modeling more seriously. He worked in clay, and his subjects were the wild animals of the West. The Greek pieces at the Metropolitan Museum inspired him to make use of their technique in his own work.

Proctor's first important commission came in 1891 from officials of the World's Columbian Exposition, which was to be held in 1893. The thirty-seven animal models he made for the exposition were highly acclaimed. He was married in 1893, and two weeks later he and his bride sailed for Paris, where Proctor attended Denys Puech's classes at the Académie Julian.

Back in New York the following year, he began to create horses for Augustus Saint Gaudens's equestrian sculptures of Gen. John Logan and Gen. William Tecumseh Sherman. His successes at the Columbian Exposition and his association with Saint-Gaudens led to widespread exposure, and his sculptures found a ready market. In 1895 he was elected to the American Academy of Design, and the following year he received the Rinehart Scholarship for three years of study in Paris. As his reputation continued to grow, he won gold medals at the 1904 St. Louis Exposition and the 1915 Panama-Pacific Exposition and sculpted heroic pieces for New York, Denver, Pittsburgh, Buffalo, Washington, D.C., and several other cities, as well as for Princeton University.

One of his last and most dramatic pieces, *Mustangs*, was installed in 1948 at the University of Texas in Austin. In his autobiography Proctor wrote: "I was born during the frontier period of the United States. . . . It colored my life and influenced me greatly. . . . I am eternally obsessed with two deep desires—one, to spend as much time as possible in the wilderness, and the other, to accomplish something worthwhile in art."

Alexander Phimister Proctor. *Bull Moose.* c. 1907. Bronze, H. 19¼"

Eli Harvey

Eli Harvey (1860-1957) was a French-trained sculptor who was an outspoken critic of the influence of French Impressionism on American art. He wrote in his autobiographical volume: "God's world is clad in beauty, beauty which uplifts the heart and inspires to high thoughts and harmonious living. Why, then, should the so-called 'modernists' so debauch line and color that the ugliness of their monstrosities tends to sensuality and degeneracy?"

Harvey was born in Clinton County, Ohio. His family were Quaker farmers, who instilled in him a reverence for the pastoral life. In 1884, he entered McMicken University in Cincinnati as an art student, and was taught by Louis T. Rebisso, who was also the mentor of Solon Borglum.

One of his first commissions came from an old Quaker who gave him seventy-five sheep for two portraits. Like many artists who became known primarily for their work in sculpture, Harvey began his career as a painter. In 1889 he went to Paris for several years of study at the Académie Julian, under Jules LeFebvre, Benjamin Constant, and Henri-Lucien Doucet; at the Académie Delécleuse, under Paul-Louis Delance and Georges Callot; and, significantly, with Emmanual Frémiet at the Jardin des Plantes, the great Paris natural-history museum.

Harvey spent two years sketching and painting the animals of the Jardin des Plantes and began to model his subjects in clay, at first as anatomy studies for his paintings. He discovered modeling to be a much more satisfying outlet for his talent than painting, and while in Paris began to concentrate on this facet of art. Between 1894 and 1901 he regularly exhibited both painting and sculpture at the Paris Salon. Harvey was represented at the Paris Centennial Exposition of 1900, the Paris-Province exhibitions, the Pan American Exposition of 1901, held in Buffalo, and exhibitions of the National Sculpture Society, to which he was elected in 1901.

His ornamental sculpture can be seen on public buildings on the East Coast and in California, where he worked in his later years. Smaller versions of his heroic pieces, such as the American elk bronze, commissioned by the Order of Elks, may be seen in museums and galleries from coast to coast. Harvey's most famous pieces are of animals. He was, to use his own words "an exponent of an art that revealed the truth and beauty which has been held as a definition of art since the time of the Greek Golden Age."

Eli Harvey. *Bull Elk.* c. 1904.
Bronze, H. 33⅞"

Hermon Atkins MacNeil

Hermon Atkins MacNeil (1866-1947) is principally known for his sculpture of Indian subjects. He was born in Chelsea, Massachusetts, and began his formal art training at the Massachusetts State Normal School in Boston. Following the pattern of his contemporaries, he studied at the École des Beaux-Arts and Académie Julian in Paris.

Although he is best known as a sculptor, MacNeil also did mural paintings for expositions in Chicago, Paris, Buffalo, and St. Louis. He was the sculptor of the Mc-Kinley Memorial in Columbus, Ohio, and of the figure of General Washington on the Washington Arch in New York. He exhibited at distinguished shows at the Chicago Art Institute, at the Pennsylvania Academy, at Belli Arti in Rome, and at the Paris Salon. MacNeil served as an instructor at the Chicago Art Institute, was a member of the National Sculpture Society, and was elected to the National Academy of Design in 1906.

Indians were always MacNeil's favorite subjects. In 1895 he and the writer Hamlin Garland undertook a promotional project for the Santa Fe Railroad, spending considerable time in the Southwest. One of his most famous sculptures, *The Sun Vow*, was done from sketches made during this period. A plaster cast in the Louvre, taken of one of the Indians Columbus had brought back to Spain from the New World, served as MacNeil's model for the principal figure.

Two of his most impressive works are heroic pieces: *Coming of the White Man*, executed for Washington Park in Portland, Oregon, and *The Pony Express*, in St. Joseph, Missouri. His *Prayer for Rain* was modeled after sketches made when he attended the Snake Dance at Gallup, New Mexico.

MacNeil was a perennial student of Classical art. He felt that "it is good to have a comprehensive knowledge of what was done before because it stimulates you and helps you to interpret your own surroundings." He remained a vital artist until his death in 1947. Toward the end of a distinguished career he wrote: "It takes hard work to arrive but it is work that I have found after fifty odd years more and more interesting as one gets where it seems rather better understood."

Hermon Atkins MacNeil. *The Sun Vow* (two views). 1913. Bronze, H. 34⅛″

Charles M. Russell

Charles Marion Russell (1864-1926) is known primarily as a painter, owing to the wide circulation his work has received in the form of prints. Yet it has been maintained that "his modeling is superior to anything he attempted in the art field." (Britzman and Adams, *Charles M. Russell, the Cowboy Artist.*) His talent as a sculptor was a natural one. Throughout his life, whether in Montana cow camps or in the New York studio of his friends Will Crawford and John Marchand, Russell was never without a lump of beeswax, which his nimble fingers modeled incessantly from sheer creative pleasure.

Russell's first piece to be cast in bronze was a small medallion showing the bust of an old Indian in bas-relief. It was cast by Roman Bronze Works of New York in 1898. His first major piece, *Smoking Up,* was modeled while he was in New York in 1903 and was cast through the Cooperative Art Society. The original copyright application for *Smoking Up,* signed by the artist, is in the collection of the Whitney Gallery of Western Art.

By 1905 three more of the artist's sculptures had been cast by Roman Bronze Works and were on sale in New York's fashionable Tiffany and Company. Fifty-three of Russell's wax and clay models were cast in bronze during his life. More than that number have been cast from other Russell models since his death.

The distinctive features of Russell's sculpture are vitality and originality. American and European sculpture has generally conformed to the Graeco-Roman Classical tradition of idealized human forms and heroic symbolism. Russell was unrestrained by Classical disciplines and fused dramatic action and a wide range of novel subjects in his sculpture. His reputation as one of the outstanding artists of the West is as applicable to his sculpture as it is to his painting.

Charles M. Russell. *Watcher of the Plains.* c. 1902. Bronze, H. 10¾". The William E. Weiss, Jr., Collection in the Whitney Gallery of Western Art

Charles M. Russell. *The Bronc Twister.* Bronze, H. 18". The William E. Weiss, Jr., Collection in the Whitney Gallery of Western Art ▶

Charles M. Russell. *The Cryer.* c. 1911. Bronze, H. 10¾". The William E Weiss, Jr., Collection in the Whitney Gallery of Western Art

Charles M. Russell. *Will Rogers.* c. 1928. Bronze, H. 11¼″. The William E. Weiss, Jr., Collection in the Whitney Gallery of Western Art

◀ Charles M. Russell. *Where the Best Riders Quit.* Bronze, H. 14½″

Charles M. Russell. *Old Napi.* Wax, H. 10⅜″

Frederic Remington

Frederic Sackrider Remington (1861-1909) was already firmly established as the leading Western illustrator when, with sculpture, he took his first step in the direction of pure art. During the summer of 1895 the sculptor Frederic W. Ruckstull was working in New Rochelle on the preliminary model for an equestrian statue of Gen. John Frederick Hartranft. Remington watched the project with great interest and, encouraged by Ruckstull, began work on the model of *The Bronco Buster,* the first of his twenty-five pieces of sculpture. Critical response to the piece was immediate and laudatory. In an article in *Harper's Weekly,* Arthur Hoeber wrote: "He has handled his clay in a masterly way, with great freedom and certainty of touch, and in a manner to call forth the surprise and admiration not only of his fellow craftsmen, but of sculptors as well."

Encouraged by acclaim and quick sales, Remington devoted part of his subsequent career to sculpture, with consistent success. He was introduced to the wonders of the cire-perdue, or lost-wax, method of bronze casting in 1901 by Riccardo Bertelli, of Roman Bronze Works in New York. A long association with Bertelli proved both personally and artistically rewarding to Remington.

Next to *The Bronco Buster,* which was a favorite of Theodore Roosevelt, Remington's most widely known sculpture was *Coming Through the Rye* (see page 274), copyrighted in 1902 and exhibited in a plaster version at the Louisiana Purchase Exposition of 1904 in St. Louis, and at the Lewis and Clark Exposition in Portland, Oregon, the following year.

In regard to his accomplishments as a sculptor, Remington said: "I have always had a feeling for mud. . . . It [sculpture] is a great art and satisfying to me, for my whole feeling is for form."

Frederic Remington. *The Horse Thief.* c. 1907. Bronze, H. 26½"

Frederic Remington. *The Rattle-snake.* c. 1905. Bronze, H. 22½"

◀ Frederic Remington. *Coming Through the Rye.*
c. 1902. Bronze, H. 27½" (one of two castings in the
collection of the Whitney Gallery of Western Art)

Frederic Remington. *The Mountain Man.*
c. 1903. Bronze, H. 28½"

left: Frederic Remington. *The Bronco Buster* (large version). c. 1905. Bronze, H. 31½″

Frederic Remington. *The Cheyenne.* c. 1901. Bronze, H. 21¼″

opposite page: Frederic Remington. *The Fallen Rider (The Wicked Pony).* c. 1898. Bronze, H. 21¾"

right and below: Frederic Remington. *The Wounded Bunkie* (two views). c. 1896. Bronze, H. 20¼"

Robert Scriver

Robert Scriver (born 1914) is one of the most highly regarded of contemporary sculptors, and there are many who consider him the best.

A Westerner who finds ample subject material for his work in his native region, Scriver was born and has lived most of his life in the small town of Browning, on the Blackfoot Indian Reservation of northwestern Montana. His commitment to excellence in art has led to extensive research into the lost-wax method of bronze casting, and to the establishment of his own foundry in Browning. Casting his own models has given Scriver complete control over his finished bronzes, a situation most sculptors are not fortunate enough to enjoy.

Among Scriver's most famous pieces is the large-scale bronze statue of rodeo champion Bill Linderman. It was commissioned by the Rodeo Cowboy's Association and is installed in the National Cowboy Hall of Fame in Oklahoma City. Since 1969, Scriver's bronzes have had annual summer exhibitions at the Whitney Gallery of Western Art. His polychrome diorama *Opening of the Blackfoot Sacred Medicine Pipe Bundle* is one of the most popular pieces in the gallery's permanent collection. It is unique in its conception.

Scriver, a member of the National Sculpture Society, the International Art Guild, and the Salmagundi Club, has exhibited successfully in Eastern, as well as Western, galleries. Completely self-taught in the methods of sculpture and independent of any "school" of art, he is an individualist, in art and in manner. He recalls growing up "in the days of hair chaps, high-heeled boots and spurs that jingled when they drug on the ground. All my friends are either cowboys or Indians. I don't know about any other kind of people."

Robert Scriver. *Opening of the Blackfoot Sacred Medicine Pipe Bundle.* 1970. Polychromed Hydrocal, H. 23⅛"

Harry Jackson

Harry Jackson is one of the very few contemporary Western artists to gain recognition beyond the West. Born in Chicago, Jackson ran away to Wyoming as a teenager and became a working cowboy on the historic Pitchfork Ranch near Cody.

He served in the Marines during World War II, then sought an art career in New York. Following a formative period in modernism, Jackson turned to the West for his inspiration and to the tenets of realism for his artistic credo.

Although he has executed many important paintings, including two major murals for the Whitney Gallery of Western Art, Jackson's reputation is based primarily on his sculpture. Important among the contemporary pieces in the permanent collection of the Whitney Gallery of Western Art are the exciting and dramatic *Stampede* and the tragic *Cowboy Burial*.

Jackson has the ability to perceive epic subjects in the life of the cowboy of the Western plains, and his interpretations of these subjects have lent substance to the entire field of contemporary Western art. Sculptures by Jackson have been among the most significant Western works produced in recent years.

Maintaining a studio in Wyoming and a studio-foundry in Italy, Jackson is one of our most dedicated contemporary American sculptors. His choice of subjects is from the West, but his treatment has attracted critical acclaim from a far wider audience. He is well grounded in the techniques of classic sculpture and is a serious student of art history. He has written an important book on "lost-wax" bronze casting and is an active member of the Cowboy Artists of America, participating in each of the group's annual exhibitions.

Harry Jackson. *Stampede.* 1959. ▶
Bronze, H. 15"

Harry Jackson. *Cowboy Burial.* ▶
1958. Bronze, H. 15½"

Conclusion

The popular acclaim given Western art in recent years has been truly phenomenal. Western art, both nineteenth century and contemporary, remains faithful to the absolutes of beauty, harmony, and taste. It reflects a temperate balance of thought, feeling, and technical procedure. Western painting was never fertile ground for faddish innovations in style. The fundamentals of classic representational painting served well the painters and sculptors of the West.

The historical contributions of the early artists of the West should not be minimized. Their pictorial documentation of a land and a way of life in many instances provides the most meaningful insight into a dramatic chapter in America's history. Verbal descriptions are somehow inadequate for presenting the full essence of our country's first thrusts beyond the Mississippi. It is through the art of the period that proud Americans can best come to appreciate the contributions of the early Westerners during this vitally important phase of their nation's development.

The Whitney Gallery of Western Art is more than just an art museum. There are important lessons to be learned from this particular gallery. It is essential for the survival of democracy that each generation be reminded of its heritage—the results of the hardships and struggles which their fathers endured to make our American way possible.

The history of Wyoming and the northern Rocky Mountain region, one of the most dramatic and colorful segments of our history, is faithfully preserved in the collection of the Whitney Gallery of Western Art. The purpose behind the collection is a realistic depiction of the past which will enable everyone to see the West as it actually was and not as it has been represented through too many years of literary and cinematic distortions.

In a world of mounting uncertainties, there are profound lessons to be learned from the heritage of the American West. It is ultimately for this reason that the Whitney Gallery of Western Art is dedicated to the perpetuation of the epic story of the development of the West. The collection as a whole, even more than the individual pieces, stands as a memorial to men, both white and red, who contributed bravely to the continuous saga of the United States. It also presents a living lesson in initiative and free enterprise, vital American qualities which are inspirations for all free people.

List of Illustrations

*Colorplates are marked with an asterisk.**

Photo Credits